W9-AEO-078

SONJA CORBITT

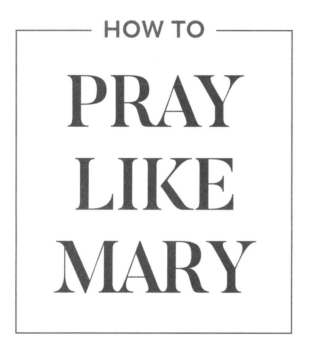

— HOW TO —

PRAY LIKE MARY

ASCENSION

West Chester, Pennsylvania

Nihil obstat: Rev. Andrew J. Bulso, S.T.L.
                   Censor librorum
                   May 10, 2019

Imprimatur: Very Rev. John J. H. Hammond, J.C.L.
                   Vicar General, Diocese of Nashville
                   May 10, 2019

Excerpts from the English translation of the *Catechism of the Catholic Church*, 2nd ed., for use in the United States of America. Copyright © 2000 United States Catholic Conference, Inc.–Libreria Editrice Vaticana. Used by permission. All rights reserved.

Unless otherwise noted, Scripture passages are from the *Revised Standard Version Bible, Second Catholic Edition.* Copyright © 2006 Division of Christian Education of the National Council of the Churches of Christ in the United States of America. Used by permission. All rights reserved.

Ascension
Post Office Box 1990
West Chester, PA 19380
1-800-376-0520
ascensionpress.com

Printed in the United States of America

ISBN 978-1-945179-49-5

CONTENTS

Dear Reader,

Perhaps you love Scripture but would like to get more from what you're reading. Maybe you have felt wary of applying Scripture to your personal life or would like guidance on how to go about it. Possibly you feel Scripture lacks any meaning for you personally; it's all old history that has nothing to do with you or your life. You might have wounds that need attention from God but you do not know how to reach him— how to "hear" God or know if he is hearing your prayers.

You are invited "to an encounter with Jesus, Word of God made flesh, as an event of grace that runs through the reading and the hearing of the Sacred Scriptures."[1] God's Word is there in the Scriptures for us. He wants us to understand his message and his promises. He wants to enter our lives and hearts through his Word. LOVE the Word®, a unique approach to praying with Scripture, will help you achieve that relationship with God through his Word that is shown to us by the Blessed Virgin Mary. Whether your search is for connection, answers, or understanding, LOVE the Word will help Scripture come to life for you on a daily basis.

Through the course of this book, we will explore Mary as the principle model of prayer, probe each of the four steps of LOVE the Word in depth, and then practice each step under Mary's guidance. My prayer is that you will learn how to love the Word like Mary, from Mary, as she teaches us to ponder the Word we hear and read through the landscape of our lives. Let's begin.

Sonja

---

[1]   John L. Allen Jr., "Synod: Final Propositions of the Synod of Bishops," *National Catholic Reporter*, October 27, 2008, prop. 9, ncronline.org/.

Chapter One

LOVE the Word®:
Lectio Without the Latin

My Relationship with Mary

As a convert to the Catholic Church from a Baptist denomination more than a decade ago, I came to most things "Catholic" the backward way. Mary, for instance. For most Catholics, Mary is a tender mother, but I had an ambivalent attitude toward her at first. My bishop once counseled me during confession that the measure of my Catholic faith is my relationship to Mary. Honestly, I left the confessional offended, because like many current and former non-Catholics, I found honoring her to be the most bewildering notion of Catholic doctrine and therefore preferred to ignore her entirely.

My bishop's statement bothered me for years until I finally went to Mary directly. My first communication to her was, *I don't get this at all. I don't get you at all. I think all the attention you get is weird. But I am willing to understand if you are willing to teach me.* I think she must have felt sorry for me, because after I placed my hand in hers, I made a breathtaking discovery that has deepened my faith in the gentlest, most motherly way. I am thrilled to share it with you in this book.

My Relationship with Scripture

In contrast to my relationship with Mary, my relationship with the Bible began long before I became Catholic. As a Baptist, I did not have sacraments or priesthood, so the only dependable way I knew to connect with God personally was through his Word, the Bible. So I embarked on a fitful attempt to establish a daily quiet time in the Scriptures.

Although it would be an understatement to say I am not a morning person, Scripture is full of exhortations to connect with God first thing:

> "O LORD, in the morning you hear my voice; in the morning I prepare a sacrifice for you, and watch" (Psalm 5:3).

> "Satisfy us in the morning with your mercy, that we may rejoice and be glad all our days" (Psalm 90:14).

> "His mercies never come to an end; they are new every morning" (Lamentations 3:22-23).

I decided to begin with the book of Proverbs, because it has thirty-one chapters, one for every day of the month. I got up before sunrise to allow thirty minutes of reading and prayer with the Lord before driving to work. Because it was predawn, those initial attempts consisted primarily of my sleeping through most of my thirty-minute allotment. *Perhaps that's why nothing is happening*, I thought, and complained to a mentor. After all, I had tried it for five whole days!

My mentor assured me that God would "show up" to meet me if I remained disciplined in prayer. I returned to the arduous, seemingly useless effort. On day twenty-six, God showed up. The Creator of the universe and lover of my soul spoke his silent Word directly into my heart through Proverbs 26:11. With a terrified thrill, I read it as spoken directly to me: *"Like a dog that returns to his vomit [Sonja] is a fool who repeats her folly."*

The shock of such a raw, almost coarse sentence appearing in God's holy Word, along with how clearly the Holy Spirit made me know he was speaking to me about myself through its earthiness, was an irresistible combination. That God says such things communicated his desire to receive me in all my own indelicate, earthy messiness, and showed me that I could *experience* his welcome as real and intimately present to me. For the first time, I felt his longing to show us through his Word how he knows and loves us more deeply than we can know and love ourselves, and he speaks to and embraces our deepest being with an omniscient, omnipresent finger of pure, gentle love. Experiencing God in the Scriptures that first day made me hungry for more, and I was amazed that he continued to meet me there. He became *personal* to me. I wanted to *know* him more. I wanted to *hear* him more. I wanted to *obey* him more. I wanted him to be proud of me.

So I sat at his feet in the Word every day, pouring out my heart, confessing my sin, laying out my problems and worries. I read through book after book and found insight after insight. "For it is precept upon precept, precept upon precept, line upon line, line upon line, here a little, there a little" (Isaiah 28:10).

My faithful, daily prayer time with the Scriptures went from thirty minutes to forty-five minutes, and then to an hour. I no longer read because I was supposed to do it, but because I wanted to discover more of the treasure God was revealing to me. When I came to passages that spoke to me, offering me hope or wisdom or insight, I savored them. I prayed over the passages and recorded them in my prayer journal. I asked God to confirm what I thought he was saying to me, and I anticipated his answers by watching the days' events.

As I grew in my understanding of Scripture and read more attentively, I realized that my faith had previously been pitifully lacking, and more intellectual than personal. I settled into a regular routine of prayer with Scripture that began to bring order to my disordered, painful life. I began to relate to him without fear as Heavenly Father. My relationship with Jesus and other people became fresh and fertile. The Holy Spirit seemed to be speaking at every turn as I discovered more about what God was like, his purposes and his ways.

As a new Catholic, I was surprised to learn that my daily quiet time was, in fact, an ancient Catholic practice, and not one my previous denomination had invented at all. My daily time with Scripture grew even more rich when I realized—to my delighted surprise—that pondering the Word of God in silence and solitude on a regular basis was also Mary's secret to deep, fruitful, powerful prayer.

MARY, MODEL OF PRAYER

In a 2012 general audience, Pope Emeritus Benedict XVI called Mary our "model for prayer," saying that her extraordinary holiness is "the result of a deep relationship with God developed in assiduous and intense prayer."[1]

---

[1]   National Catholic Register, *Pope Benedict: Mary Is Our Model for Prayer*, March 14, 2012, ncregister.com/.

This deep relationship with God, he said, is characterized by her capacity to maintain an uninterrupted state of contemplation by meditating on events before God in the silence of her heart. He pointed out how God particularly placed Mary at the decisive moment of salvation history, and how she was able to respond with full availability precisely *because* she pondered events and circumstances in her heart with him. Her full availability incarnated the Word and shared him with the world.

After the Ascension, Mary continued to share Jesus with the disciples through the most precious of her possessions: her living memory of him. The apostles' poignant sharing and waiting in expectant prayer *with Mary* brought forth the presence and power of the Holy Spirit, tongues of fire that set the world aflame. If it was true then, how much truer is it for us?

Mary connects us deeply to the Holy Spirit, just as she did the apostles, through her process of listening and pondering. She teaches us the *one thing necessary* (see Luke 10:38-42) through her unique way of prayer; she models for us how to *love* the Word. She shows us that it is only through "a constant, intimate, wholly loving bond with her Son that we can leave 'our house' ... and proclaim everywhere the Lord Jesus, Savior of the world."[2]

MARY PRAYS SCRIPTURE

When Mary prayed, she expressed herself, in part, with Scripture! She showed us this in offering the Magnificat as a song of thanksgiving verbalized to God in Elizabeth's

---

[2] Benedict XVI, "Mary and Prayer," in *A School of Prayer: The Saints Show Us How to Pray* (San Francisco: Ignatius Press, 2013), n. 29.

presence. As a devout Jewish woman, Mary would have prayed all her life for the coming of the Jewish Messiah. Now God had answered her prayer—shockingly—through Mary herself (see Luke 1:46-55). Based on the earlier Song of Hannah (1 Samuel 2:1-10), Mary's song shows her intimacy with and love of Scripture. Both songs demonstrate the parallelism of Hebrew poetry and psalmody. Mary was so familiar with Scripture that her Magnificat echoes both Hannah's song and the psalms of the Old Testament.

Hannah's song was also a song of joy and praise. Hannah—like Abraham's wife Sarah—had been barren, but in old age both women conceived by God's promise. Sarah became the mother of Isaac and all those with faith (see Genesis 17, 18, and 22), and Hannah became the mother of the prophet Samuel.

Both Sarah and Hannah—barren women who became unlikely mothers—can be seen as types, or foreshadowings, of Mary, although the miracle of Mary's motherhood was due to her virginity, not barrenness. Mary is the culmination of God's work through all the women who fulfilled Isaiah's prophecy, "'Sing, O barren one, who did not bear; break forth into singing and cry aloud, you who have not had labor pains! For the children of the desolate one will be more than the children of her that is married,' says the LORD" (Isaiah 54:1).

In his letter to the Galatians, St. Paul uses this passage from Isaiah to liken the Church to Sarah's children—children of the promise (see Galatians 4:26-27). As the fulfillment of Sarah, Mary freely embraced Jesus and became mother and symbol of the Church through him (see Revelation 12). The Church, as mother, embraces all who embrace Christ.

For these reasons the Church has used these passages in worship liturgy to speak of Mary since the very beginning. Each of these passages—Sarah's story, Hannah's song, Isaiah's prophecy, the Magnificat, and Paul's letter to the Galatians—all "rejoice" in a "barren" woman who gives birth to a promise of God. Mary is the New Sarah, the New Hannah, the New Jerusalem personified. Mary is the Mother of the Church (see Revelation 12:13-17) through the Word of God.

We too can pray the Scriptures and acclimate ourselves to them until they become what prophetically erupts from our hearts and lips at any given moment. We can adjust our practice and spirit to God's Word so that it gets us outside of ourselves and into the flow of what the Holy Spirit is already achieving in the Church, which he has been building and nurturing for millennia.

Mary's practice of *being with* the Word, where one lets go of one's own agenda in reading and opens oneself to what God wants to say, is at the heart of a method of praying that the Church has known and taught for centuries under the name *lectio divina*, which is Latin for "divine reading." Scripture will come alive for us and make us bearers of Christ into the world when we begin approaching it as God's direct Word to us about our individual lives, circumstances, and problems.

The saints have always said the best place to begin in the Scriptures is to pray with them.

THE HISTORY OF PRAYER WITH THE SCRIPTURES

Early Prayer with Scripture

At the Creation of the cosmos, God's Word brought forth life. Later, "in many and various ways God spoke of old to our fathers by the prophets" (Hebrews 1:1). When spiritual re-creation was on the horizon, God again sent forth his Word to a single person who already had a habit of connecting to it.

I like to picture Mary praying as described by Anne Catherine Emmerich, an eighteenth-century German stigmatic whose visions inspired parts of the 2004 movie *The Passion of the Christ*. Emmerich envisioned Mary in her private chamber, praying specifically for the Messiah promised to her people when the announcement that *she* would be the mother of the Messiah came to her through the angel.[3] It's just as likely that Mary received God's Word from the angel amid the pots and pans of her duties and station in life. But Emmerich's private revelation of Mary praying in her chamber makes sense to me, in part because, for Jews of Mary's time, every day belonged to God and many hours were devoted to prayer. As a faithful Jewish girl, Mary would have prayed daily on her own and with her family.

Mary's practice of daily prayer would have begun before Christ was born. But long before Mary, the Israelites did the same. In the earliest years of Jewish history, no set prayer order or prayer form existed. Individuals prayed as often as and in whatever words and posture they chose. However, after Moses' lifetime, a set order of service developed as part of morning and evening sacrifices in the tabernacle.

---

[3] Anne Catherine Emmerich, *The Life of the Blessed Virgin Mary*, trans. Michael Palairet (Charlotte, NC: TAN Books, 2011), 141–147.

Later, at the Temple in Jerusalem, the prayers extended even after the evening sacrifice, later into the night.

After the exile, when the Jews returned to their homeland, the prophets and priests standardized Scripture passages and established three daily readings as a requirement for daily Jewish prayers. Daily, fixed-hour prayer was thus born and flourished, and special prayers for the Sabbath and other feasts and festivals were added.

This pattern continued, as shown in the Old Testament, developing into the practice of praying three times a day at specific hours. David (see Psalm 55:17) and Daniel (see Daniel 6:10) are examples, while Jeremiah gives us a glimpse into the public prayer space ("the house of the people," Jeremiah 39:8) dedicated to this sacrificial prayer practice in the first Temple. Ezekiel prophesied that there would be such prayer spaces designated for fixed-hour prayers in the Messianic temple, the New Testament church (see Ezekiel 37:26-38).

The Jewish prayers were indeed carried forward into the New Testament. For instance, the people prayed the prescribed passages of Scripture outside while Zechariah offered incense inside the Temple at the "hour of incense" (Luke 1:10). The apostles also fulfilled Ezekiel's prophecy of prayer times and spaces, as told in the book of Acts (3:1), where we see they observed the traditional hours of prayer, even going to the Temple to do so, until they were excommunicated for their Christian faith.

For the early Christians, morning prayer coincided with the morning sacrifice observed at the Temple in Jerusalem at the third hour, or nine o'clock in the morning (see Acts 2:15).

Midday prayer was at the sixth hour, or noon, and may have coincided with the thanksgiving blessing for the chief meal of the day (see Matthew 15:36; Acts 27:35). Evening prayer was paired with the evening sacrifice, at the ninth hour, or three o'clock in the afternoon (see Acts 3:1, 10:30).

The Liturgy of the Hours

Eventually this way of praying with Scripture throughout the day was named the Liturgy of the Hours, or the Divine Office. The Word "liturgy" is from the Greek word *leitourgia*, meaning "a work of the people," a public worship ceremony or ritual. Based on the fixed-hour prayers of Judaism, the Liturgy of the Hours, then (in its widest application), is the formal daily and yearly cycle that characterizes communal Christian prayer for the Catholic and Orthodox churches and the liturgical denominations. It is a way of "keeping time" with God that reflects and carries forward the fixed-hour prayers of Judaism.

The traditional Christian hours are:

- Lauds (sunrise prayer, or "praises")
- Prime (6:00 AM, morning prayer)
- Terce (9:00 AM, mid-morning prayer)
- Sext (noon or midday prayer)
- None (3:00 PM, afternoon prayer)
- Vespers (sunset, evening prayer)
- Compline (bedtime, night prayer)

This ancient prayer practice that reaches all the way back to ancient Judaism—which Mary would have known and taught Jesus to pray—connects us to God and to one another with God's Word even today. Following the entire schedule ensures that you will pray all 150 psalms once each month. The readings from the Liturgy of the Hours and the Mass together cover the whole New Testament every year and include Old Testament readings that are important in salvation history.

When you consider the staggered time zones across the world, it's easy to understand how, in the Catholic Church, the Liturgy of the Hours and the Mass are being prayed somewhere at every moment, as the clergy, diaconate, and religious orders commit to these daily, fixed-hour prayers on behalf of the universal Church every single day. As non-Jews keeping this discipline, the Church fulfills both Ezekiel's Messianic temple prophecy and Malachi's prophecy, "For from the rising of the sun to its setting my name is great among the nations, and in every place incense is offered to my name, and a pure offering" (Malachi 1:11).

The Liturgy of the Hours is truly interdenominational, because the prayers consist almost entirely of Holy Scripture. Praying these prayers is reading and praying Scripture with the mind of the Church. It keeps us in tune with what the Holy Spirit is creating and renewing in the universal Church, just as their daily prayers kept Mary and the apostles connected to his active, creative Word in their day.

If this is the first you've heard of such a discipline, you may consider it onerous or oppressive, but the practice is done with great love and devotion all over the world. Ongoing for millennia, this structured prayer for God's people continues to be the backbone of worship for the whole Church community. Without it, prayer would become an individual pick-and-choose practice that connects individuals to no one.

The full Liturgy of the Hours is rather demanding, since it involves pausing seven times a day for ten to fifteen minutes each time. My lay duties and station in life allow me to keep the practice by praying the morning prayers, Mass, and evening prayers all at once. Except for hymns, intercessions, and readings from the Church fathers and the saints, the Liturgy of the Hours is entirely scriptural, which means I hear from the Holy Spirit in the Scriptures every day, and so does every other Christian who keeps the practice.

For me, reaching that goal came through the discipline and practice developed through a heart of love and a longing to know God. When I was just beginning, when my discipline had progressed to the necessary stage, simple willpower had to kick in so I could push through the predictable seasons of dryness. However, the exciting news is that when I stay with the discipline, God shows up.

The Development of Lectio Divina

After the apostles were excommunicated and the Temple in Jerusalem was destroyed, Origen of Alexandria (AD 184–253), a Christian theologian of the early Church, is thought to have introduced a more conversational, contemplative practice of prayer with Scripture. His idea was more "Scripture as a sacrament" through which *Jesus* speaks, touches, and teaches. No one really knows who named the practice *lectio divina* (Latin for "sacred reading" or "divine reading"), but the process has always been more about *experiencing* the Word than about studying it for knowledge or praying it in liturgy.

Classical *lectio divina* began before Bibles were printed, as a monastic practice of communal prayer when Benedictine brothers gathered at chapel each day. Because the printing press wasn't invented until the 1400s, no one was able to read Scripture independently because of their rarity and immense value. Until then, Bibles were hand copied by monks and often chained to an ambo, or pulpit, to prevent theft. Personal copies did not exist, and illiteracy was so pervasive that only the wealthy and educated could have read one. So instead, the Benedictine brothers gathered to listen to the readings. They felt the Spirit and understood that they were hearing the Word of God, much as Mary heard God's Word through the angel. They listened to Scripture with their hearts, as the Word of God, "squeezing from it, so to speak, all its 'juice,' so that it may nourish meditation and contemplation and, like water, succeed in irrigating life itself," as Pope Benedict described it.[4]

Later, in the twelfth century, the stages classically considered essential to *lectio divina* were formalized into four steps: *lectio* ("reading"), *meditatio* ("meditation"), *oratio* ("prayer"), and *contemplatio* ("contemplation"). *Lectio divina* continues to be, as Pope Benedict called it, "a wellspring of constant renewal" in the Church.[5]

YOU, MARY, AND SCRIPTURE

According to Pope Benedict, praying like Mary is more than simply hearing or reading the Word. Mary is the "model for prayer," the mother of prayer with the Word, because of her "deep bond with God that developed in assiduous and intense prayer."[6] Mary's lifelong, personal practice of

---

[4] Benedict XVI, Sunday Angelus (November 6, 2005), vatican.va/.

[5] Benedict XVI, *Verbum Domini*, Post-synodal Apostolic Exhortation on the Word of God in the Life and Mission of the Church (September 30, 2010), vatican.va/.

[6] Benedict XVI, "Without Mary There Is No Church," general audience, March 14, 2012, *L'Osservatore Romano*, March 21, 2012, 3, available at etwn.com/.

attentive listening shows how practically and beautifully she illustrated the traditional steps of *lectio divina*. She would have prayed with the Word, and she loved the Word of God so that it came alive within her and was born into the world. As we will see, she guides us with a sure hand in how to do the same.

Like Our Lady, we actively seek a deep relationship with God in his Word on a daily basis as a spiritual discipline. We ponder circumstances and events in his presence so that we can entrust them all to him and remain in an attitude of deep peace. *Come, Holy Spirit.* As was true for Mary, the Word that we hear and read today is a gift from God in answer to our prayers. Our lives throb with gratitude and joy, and burst with anticipation for all we encounter.

When we use the method that the Church has known and taught for centuries, and follow Mary's example of listening and entrusting—when we begin approaching the readings as God's Word to us, direct communication to us about our individual lives—Scripture will come alive for us and make us bearers of Christ into the world.

The saints have always said that the best way to begin in Scripture is to pray with them in *lectio divina*, but the ancient Latin terms can make *lectio* seem more inaccessible than it is. Therefore, we will learn and practice a method without the Latin, using a simple acronym modeled on her Annunciation:

L–LISTEN, **O**–OBSERVE, **V**–VERBALIZE, **E**–ENTRUST

Pope Saint Paul VI stated that "in the sacred books, the Father who is in heaven meets his children with great love and speaks with them; and the force and power in the Word of God is so great that it stands as the support and energy of the Church, the strength of faith for her sons, the food of the soul, the pure and everlasting source of spiritual life."[7]

Indeed, the Scriptures have always been part of the "one table" of the Lord that animates and nourishes the life of the believer:

> The Church has always venerated the Scriptures as she venerates the Lord's Body. She never ceases to present to the faithful the bread of life, taken from the *one table* of God's Word and Christ's Body.
>
> In Sacred Scripture, the Church constantly finds her nourishment and her strength, for she welcomes it not as a human word, "but as what it really is, the word of God." In the sacred books, the Father who is in heaven comes lovingly to meet his children, and talks with them. (CCC 103–104, emphasis added)

We may not be called to engage in the entire demanding schedule of fixed-hour prayer in order to be intimate with the Holy Spirit, but Mary models and the Church teaches that daily nourishment in the Scriptures is an absolute necessity. Following Mary's example with disciplined and consistent prayer and joining with the worldwide Church community through the Mass readings particularly invites and facilitates God's powerful action in our lives. Mary demonstrated that intimacy with the Holy Spirit occurs through praying with Scripture.

Because she prayed the prayers of her people, Mary had assimilated the Old Testament Scriptures so completely that when she opened her mouth to praise God, what erupted as

---

7   Paul VI, *Dei verbum* (November 18, 1965), vatican.va/.

praise was Scripture.[8] Her spontaneous song of gratitude for God's miraculous answer to her prayers is the crown of Old Testament prayer and Scripture, the last of the Old Testament and the first of the New Testament.

Because Mary, as the mother of Jesus, our Savior, was the first to experience and extend salvation to the world, she is also an icon of both ancient Israel and the universal Church. Every soul, whether male or female, *receives* from God, so regardless of gender or temperament, Mary is our model of prayer with the Word.

When I asked Mary to help me understand my bishop's assertion that my relationship to her is the measure of my Catholic faith, I had no idea that her singing heart would reveal the Holy Spirit's own intense desire for, and invitation to, a deeper, more consuming intimacy with me. Your own desire to pray like Mary is her invitation to a deeper intimacy with the Holy Spirit.

As we allow our "mother of prayer" to guide us, we discover how usefully and beautifully she helps us pray the Scriptures. Mary teaches us how to begin, sustain, deepen, and anticipate hearing God speak through his Word on a daily basis. Mary loves the Word of God so that it comes alive within her and is born into the world, and she guides us with love in how to do the same. In the coming chapters, we will learn the steps.

---

[8] Jesus did something similar in his frequent application of certain Scriptures to his ministry and specific actions, especially the psalms he prayed from the Cross.

LET'S REVIEW

Let's review what Mary teaches us about prayer.

- *Mary is calling us* to deeper prayer through the Scriptures.
- "*The Church has always venerated the Scriptures* as she venerates the Lord's Body" (CCC 103, emphasis added).
- *Sacred Scripture is the Word of God* (see CCC 104).
- *God is always speaking* through his Word.
- *We can follow the example Mary set* during the Annunciation through the pattern of LOVE the Word: **L**–listen, **O**–observe, **V**–verbalize, **E**–entrust.
- If we commit to a daily discipline in LOVE the Word, *God promises to speak* there.

INVITATION

St. Augustine once said of his relationship with the Lord, "Late have I loved thee."[9] I came to a Catholic relationship with Mary and the Bible late, but under Mary's guidance, my prayer practice has developed a singular power that nourishes me and propels me forward in my life. In following her lead, she is answering my most constant, fervent prayer: *Lord, I just want to be a fire in your hand.*

As we embark on the most exciting endeavor of our lives, seeking God's face in the Scriptures every day, "may Our

---

9   Augustine of Hippo, *Confessions* (Indianapolis, IN: Hackett, 2006), 210.

Lady teach us to welcome the Word of God fully, not only through intellectual research, but in our whole life."[10]

GOD PROMPT
Practice LOVE the Word®

Invite the Holy Spirit to speak to you through the following passage from Proverbs 26:11, then read the passage slowly and reflectively (with full attention), emphasizing one word of the verse in turn until you have stressed them all. This will help the words to really sink in. Consider reading the passage aloud.

L–Listen *(Receive the Word.)*

"**Like** a dog that returns to his vomit is a fool who repeats his folly."

"Like a **dog** that returns to his vomit is a fool who repeats his folly."

"Like a dog that **returns** to his vomit is a fool who repeats his folly."

"Like a dog that returns to **his** vomit is a fool who repeats his folly."

"Like a dog that returns to his **vomit** is a fool who repeats his folly."

"Like a dog that returns to his vomit **is** a fool who repeats his folly."

---

[10] Pope Francis, Address to the Italian Biblical Association (September 12, 2014), vatican.va/.

O–Observe (*Place yourself in the narrative, imagining every detail.*)

My "vomit" is rage. What is your "vomit"? What dirty, disgusting, or foolish habit or relationship do you instinctively return to over and over again? Have you done so recently? What is God saying to you about that destructive, instinctive behavior through this verse?

V–Verbalize (*Pray about your thoughts and emotions.*)

What does he want you to do now? Spend a few moments talking to God about the feelings and thoughts that arise in your heart right now.

E–Entrust (*May it be done to me according to your Word!*)

Perhaps you'd like to simply rest in God's presence for a moment and entrust your future to him anew.

Chapter Two

Step 1: L–Listen

In an address in St. Peter's Square, Pope Francis compared our ability to pray the Word generatively with Our Lady's, calling Mary the "mother of listening":

> What gave rise to Mary's act of going to visit her relative Elizabeth? A *word* of God's Angel. "Elizabeth in her old age has also conceived a son ..." (Luke 1:36). Mary knew how to listen to God. Be careful: it was not merely "hearing" a superficial Word, but it was "listening," that consists of attention, acceptance and availability to God. It was not in the distracted way with which we sometimes face the Lord or others: we hear their words, but we do not really listen. Mary is attentive to God. She listens to God.
>
> However Mary also listens to the events, that is, she interprets the events of her life, she is attentive to reality itself and does not stop on the surface but goes to the depths to grasp its meaning. Her kinswoman Elizabeth, who is already elderly, is expecting a child: this is the event. But Mary is attentive to the meaning. She can understand it: "with God nothing will be impossible" (Luke 1:37).
>
> This is also true in our life: listening to God who speaks to us, and listening also to daily reality, paying attention to people, to events, because the Lord is at the door of our life and knocks in many ways, he puts signs on our path;

he gives us the ability to see them. Mary is the mother of listening, of attentive listening to God and of equally attentive listening to the events of life.[1]

Therein lies the outline for praying like Mary. First, Mary *listens* to God, personally, in habitual attention, acceptance, and availability.

MARY, MOTHER OF LISTENING

Is "listening" simply reading the Scriptures? If I read passage after passage, book after book of the Bible, have I really prayed if I have not discerned God as a Person there and adjusted my life to what I have heard?

Listening to God then, as Mary practices it, is prayer most fully in God's presence, an attitude of orientation toward God, of sensing God and receiving him as a personal "holy other" in wonder and adoration. Perhaps the first thing we must do to really listen is to invite him to speak: *Speak, Lord, for your servant is listening.*

The Word of God is the Person of Christ, not a book (see John 1). But that one Word is the subject of all Scripture. The Bible is a holy book precisely because God speaks to us through it; it is his personal Word to us. In order to reveal himself to us, he speaks through human words (see CCC 101–104). When I come to the Scriptures, the Holy Spirit himself is present to speak to me.

Because Sacred Scripture extends from the genesis of the cosmos to its apocalypse, God has always been and always is speaking. We simply do not listen: "Today, when you hear his voice, do not harden your hearts" (Hebrews 3:15).

---

[1]   Francis, Recital of the Holy Rosary for the Conclusion of the Marian Month of May (May 31, 2013), n. 1, vatican.va/, emphasis added.

Every day is today. Throughout the Bible, we learn how God has revealed himself, his purposes, and his ways to humanity in the past. We read those accounts of God's dealings with his people throughout salvation history in order to know him, his purposes, and his ways with *us*. To Mary he committed the beginning of his gospel from the announcement of the angel to the birth and infancy of the Son of God made man. It is with Mary that Jesus' earthly life begins and with Mary, too, that the Church takes her first steps; both these moments are steeped in an atmosphere of listening to God, of recollection.[2] It is because of her inner attitude of listening that Mary can interpret her own story, humbly recognizing that it is the Lord who is acting.[3]

The "gospel," or *good news*, is freedom in Christ. If we are not listening to God on a daily basis, how will we know him and his purpose and way with us? How will *we* ever be free from the "vomit"—the destructive habits, relationships, and repeating circumstances that prevent us from living abundantly and serving God fully? If we cannot live abundantly and serve God fully, we cannot fulfill the unique purpose and expression we were created for.

Jesus told the Pharisees, "He who is of God hears the words of God; the reason why you do not hear them is that you are not of God" (John 8:47). The Pharisees had outward religion: They went through the motions, they kept the rituals, they said the prayers, but their hearts were far from God (see Matthew 15:8) because they were not *listening* to him: "Why do you not understand what I say? It is because you cannot bear to hear my word" (John 8:43).

---

2   Benedict XVI, "Without Mary There Is No Church."
3   Ibid.

Are we afraid of what God might say to us? Is that why we do not carve out time for listening?

According to Pope Francis, listening like Mary is more than simply hearing or reading the Word. Mary is the "mother of listening" because she is attentive and available to God. Like Our Lady, I am attentive by opening my heart to *receive* the Word of God, by accepting "it not as the word of men but as what it really is, the word of God" (1 Thessalonians 2:13).

In order to pray like Mary, we approach the Scriptures as God's personal word to us every day. We begin listening by praying or saying aloud, "Holy Spirit, what do you want to say to me through this passage?" And then, like Mary, we wait with attention to see what he says.

LISTENING REQUIRES SILENCE

We must be quiet in order to make room for the Word, for our human words are ridiculous compared to the one Eternal Word. "Silence is the language of God—sanctity's mother tongue," according to Lawrence Lovasik, SVD, missionary priest and founder of the Family Service Corps.[4] Learning to be comfortable and still in silence is possibly the most important thing we can foster in the spiritual life, as true listening can only happen in silence.

Did you know that *silent* and *listen* are the same letters in a different order? We need both to focus with attention—the silence of no distraction and the ability to listen without interruption. The noise in our lives and homes and in

---

[4]   Lawrence G. Lovasik, *The Hidden Power of Kindness* (Manchester, NH: Sophia Institute Press, 1999), 173.

the world is endless and sometimes deafening. Silence is displaced by music and voices and social media and the twenty-four-hour news cycle. How will we ever hear God speak if we cannot be silent? Listening is silence.

In an interview about his spiritual meditation on silence, Robert Cardinal Sarah argues that silence is the only way God allows himself to be approached. God is silence. We were created in the silence of his image. He waits for our silence to reveal himself, so silence is necessarily a matter of proper priorities. Sarah goes so far as to say that noise can be "diabolical":

> Our busy, ultra-technological age has made us even sicker. Noise has become like a drug on which our contemporaries are dependent. With its festive appearance, noise is a whirlwind that avoids looking oneself in the face and confronting the interior emptiness. It is a diabolical lie.[5]

It is therefore in the struggle for silence that we find true freedom. As Cardinal Sarah explains, silence "leads us toward God and toward others so that we can place ourselves humbly at their service." He calls the need to encounter God in silence an "urgent necessity" and "more important than any other human work" because "it expresses God."[6] Not a pause between two rituals, silence is ritual itself. Silence is discipline. In silence, we are renewed.

SILENCE ENFLAMED

Trappists, rocket scientists, popes, professors—no matter how intellectual or intensely devout one is, without

---

5   "Cardinal Robert Sarah on 'The Strength of Silence' and the Dictatorship of Noise," interview by French newspaper *La Nef*, trans. Michael J. Miller, *Catholic World Report*, October 3, 2016, catholicworldreport.com/.
6   Ibid.

intentional silence, there can be no focus, no recollection. Our doctors of prayer tell us that recollection is constant attention of the mind and affections of the heart to thoughts and sentiments which elevate the soul to God.[7] We might even call this recollection wisdom, or the gift and promise of God's perspective on our circumstances and relationships, the reality of how they truly are: "If any of you lacks wisdom, let him ask God, who gives to all men generously and without reproaching, and it will be given him" (James 1:5).

There is a silence called *exterior recollection* by the mystic doctors of prayer, in which we put ourselves in a place of quiet and allow the mind to wander and rest—a "wandering silence" in which meditation and rumination occur. When we "enter" this silence in LOVE the Word®, we leave the details of our day aside and let our minds drift freely over the Scripture we have read or heard. This type of listening occurs in our *O–observe* step, which we will probe in the next chapter.

Until then, as you listen, perhaps you go to your prayer corner to examine the daily readings, focusing on the reading and then letting your mind wander, noticing the images that form and the feelings they produce. Or you take a walk or sit quietly in a chapel, listening to the silence and letting it restore your soul, allowing the Word you have read to become present within you (see Psalm 23). Perhaps while you are with the Lord in this way, you bring him your needs and hopes, and maybe in that moment you ask him to provide for you according to the passage you just read.

---

7   Arthur Devine, "State or Way (Purgative, Illuminative, Unitive)," in *The Catholic Encyclopedia* (New York: Robert Appleton, 1912), available at newadvent.org/.

Our doctors of prayer say that alternately focusing the mind and letting it wander in this way, and the accompanying feeling of fluctuating sweetness and lack of sweetness, is the listening proper to the long-term purgative and illuminative stages of prayer, where we cooperate with God to actively clear our lives of sin and noise, and struggle to practice virtue.[8]

As we learn to pray using the LOVE the Word, we seek silence. This can be the silence of "a place apart"—our prayer space, our favorite walk, or a seat by the fire. Or it may be the silence we enter as we do ordinary things during the day. Folding the laundry, changing the oil, washing the dishes, cutting the grass, and weeding the garden can all become inhabited with Presence as we ponder the Word in silence with Mary. Our duties are not necessarily impediments to silence, then, but directions and steps. In the novelist George Eliot's words, "If we had a keen vision of all ordinary human life, it would be like hearing the grass grow and the squirrel's heart beat, and we should die of that roar which lies on the other side of silence."[9]

DEEPENING THE SILENCE

To remain always focused on our day-to-day lives is to forfeit a deeper reality, the richer silence, in whom "we live and move and have our being" (Acts 17:28). This is why Jesus taught that the intrusive noise and weeds of life can choke out the real thing (see Mark 4:1–9), the life he promises us. Beneath our busyness, responsibilities, anxieties, dreams,

---

8   John of the Cross, "The Dark Night," in *The Collected Works of St. John of the Cross*, trans. Kieran Kavanaugh and Otilio Rodriguez (Washington, DC: ICS Publications, 1991), 358–457 .

9   George Eliot, *Middlemarch* (Lexington, KY: Digireads, 2016), 151-152.

and problems, there is a deeper and vastly more authentic reality, the Word whose presence we seek in our prayer.

But the concerns of each day are hard to dismiss. Isn't it true that as soon as we attempt to focus and connect in solitude and silence, thoughts, ideas, and memories ping our attention away in a cascade of related distractions? Aren't we in a perpetual self-dialogue of critiquing and classifying the people and circumstances we experience? "'How well am I doing?' 'Is it safe here?' 'What did she mean by that?' 'Am I okay?'" [10] Our awareness of reality occurs mostly at this superficial level of awareness.

Our doctors of prayer call disciplined detachment from the constant self-talk in our minds *interior recollection*. It is a focused attention, a "deep and delicate listening,"[11] the purposeful entering into solitude and quiet. Only the physical *and* mental slowing of silence and stillness can develop this deeper shift, found in connecting to the Presence within that helps me see as he sees. St. John of the Cross maintains, "God speaks to the heart in this solitude ... while the soul listens."[12]

IN THE WOMB OF SILENCE

Our purposeful solitude opens the way to the mystical silence within, populated with the explosive intimacy that made Moses cram himself between the rocks as the Silence engulfed him (see Exodus 33:22).

---

[10] Cynthia Bourgeault, "Silence Is God's First Language," November 2004, beliefnet.com/.

[11] John of the Cross, "The Living Flame of Love," in Kavanaugh and Rodriguez, *Collected Works*, 687.

[12] Ibid.

When attempting to transition from outer silence to inner silence, we are accustomed to our minds constantly thinking, puzzling, planning, observing, and questioning, so when we sit in uninterrupted quiet without processing something, we may feel inadequate, as if nothing is happening or we are wasting time. Our minds will wander or be plagued with questions, unused to the act of sinking into the deeper, darker silence. You may wonder if you're doing something wrong when you don't get an immediate flood of inspiration or reflection.

Saints suggest selecting a single word to bring ourselves back to focus when the mind wanders—*Lord, Help,* or *Jesus*— something short and pointed in order to quickly return us to seeking God in the silence:

> To refuse this silence filled with confident awe and adoration is to refuse God the freedom to capture us by his love and his presence. Sacred silence is therefore the place where we can encounter God, because we come to him with the proper attitude of a human being who trembles and stands at a distance while hoping confidently. ... Saint John Paul II warns us: a human being enters into participation in the divine presence "above all by letting himself be educated in an adoring silence, because at the summit of the knowledge and experience of God there is his absolute transcendence."[13]

What happens in the dark womb of silence over time is complete rebirth. In receiving the Word of God this way, Mary began, in a sense, her Son's renewal of the entire human race.

Jesus often taught that we must let ourselves be transformed: "You must be born anew" (John 3:7), "Unless a grain of

---

13   Sarah, interview in *Catholic World Report.*

wheat falls into the earth and dies, it remains alone; but if it dies, it bears much fruit" (John 12:24), and "For whoever would save his life will lose it, and whoever loses his life for my sake will find it" (Matthew 16:25).[14] According to two millennia of saints, pure prayer tends irrevocably to the total transformation of the person, drawing us out of superficial illusion and into the deeper reality. Maybe more than any other requirement, silence as spiritual practice is essential to spiritual rebirth and transformation. In silence and solitude we hear the voice of God. "Therefore, behold, I will allure her, and bring her into the wilderness, and speak tenderly to her" (Hosea 2:14).

Perhaps establishing a fruitful listening practice is based primarily in wanting to do so in the first place, so let us reflect on that. Consider a practice of forty days.

FORTY DAYS' GESTATION

God cleansed the earth with a flood that lasted forty days and forty nights (see Genesis 7:12); Moses lived in the desert forty years before his call (see Acts 7:29-30) and spent forty days and forty nights on Mount Sinai with God, receiving the Ten Words and the Law (see Exodus 34:28); Moses and the Israelites wandered in the desert for forty years (see Numbers 14:34); Goliath taunted Israel forty days (see 1 Samuel 17:16); Elijah fasted and prayed on Mount Horeb for forty days (see 1 Kings 19:8); Ezekiel lay on his side for forty days as a prophetic gesture (see Ezekiel 4:6); the people of Nineveh fasted for forty days after Jonah's warning (see Jonah 3:4); and Jesus fasted and prayed for forty days and nights in the desert in preparation for his public ministry

---

[14]   Bourgeault, "Silence Is God's First Language," 2.

(see Luke 4:2). Our penitential Lenten season follows this pattern as a forty-day observance.

Perhaps most relevant in our consideration of how to pray like Mary is that she incubated the Word in her womb for forty weeks.

The number forty is a Jewish literary device used throughout the Bible that means something like "the perfect length of time." Spiritually speaking, forty is the number of gestation. In order to give birth to a new LOVE the Word habit, we should plan to spend forty days cultivating it.

Living things grow in a womb of silence. So, too, gestation of a prayer habit with the Scriptures occurs in forty days of silence.

BEFORE THE FACE

The point of prayer, then, is that it is a daily moment that culminates in a lifetime of silent, intimate encounter in which a human being stands face to Face with God and allows him to speak. Once we are comfortable with silence and make it a daily practice, silence becomes an attitude of the soul.

Cardinal Sarah speaks profoundly and prophetically when he says that without face-to-Face silence, we continue in illusion.[15] The threat of Jesus' teaching was precisely the unmasking of our comfortable, noisy illusions in the silent face to Face with him. Like the red pill Morpheus offers Neo in the movie *The Matrix*, the "threat" of truth and freedom remains, daily, in God's Word: "If you continue in my word, you are truly my disciples, and you will know the truth, and the truth will make you free" (John 8:31-32).

---

[15] Robert Sarah, *The Power of Silence: Against the Dictatorship of Noise* (San Francisco: Ignatius Press, 2017), no. 15, pp. 28–29.

HOW TO LISTEN

When the Word of God came to Mary, she was said to be in her chamber, alone, praying the prayer God would answer with *her*. God answered Mary's prayer for the promised Messiah through her. She was praying for the answer, and God answered through *her*. How many times has God intended or desired to answer my prayer using *me*, but I was unavailable or inattentive to his voice and will?

How will I hear him in the noise of babies, rush-hour traffic, copy machines, business phone calls and meetings, then dinner, and bedtime and bath time and ... life? I wonder if Mary "lost" or gave up her habit of silence and solitude with God once Jesus was born.

Your strategy for prayer time must be clear. Upon awakening, take your coffee or tea and go to your prayer space. Finding a peaceful hour in the morning may require some rearrangement of your time and duties. You may need to prepare presentations, lunches, or wardrobe details before bed at night so your prayer time is not pushed aside for morning "emergencies." Perhaps you can go to bed earlier in order to rise an hour earlier, while the house is still quiet with everyone still asleep. You will have to guard this time if you're going to have it at all, and God will bless your effort if you stay with it. Envision yourself like Mary, available to God in daily solitude and regularity as a spiritual discipline, and attentive to him with an open heart, ready to receive the transformative Word of God from the Holy Spirit.

Next, Mary shows us that listening means nothing if it is not met with acceptance.

ACCEPTANCE MEANS OBEDIENCE

One of the first matters the Lord brought to my attention with the Scriptures during my morning prayer time with him was a cigarette habit held over from my late teens. The verse he used to motivate me to quit smoking was, "If you love me, you will keep my commandments" (John 14:15). The implication at the time was that I did not really love him because I had not done what he asked in making my body a temple for his Spirit (see 1 Corinthians 6:19). Because I really did love him (the best I could at that time), I formulated a strategy, tried several times, and eventually quit smoking.

Years later, when my youngest son was about eight, I became frustrated at his habitual disinterest in brushing his teeth. Every day I would remind him, and every day he would "forget." Usually my patience ended abruptly in the close proximity of a church pew: either his breath assaulted me during the entrance hymn, or the fur on his teeth reached out and waved at me at the sign of peace. I finally went to God about it during my morning prayer. Who else but the perfect parent would I ask about parenting issues? *How should I handle this in the gentlest but firmest possible way?* I asked, and as I listened for his answer, he answered my question with another question: *How do I do it with you?*

Immediately the verse from my smoking days sprang to mind: "If you love me, you will keep my commandments" (John 14:15). Inspired by my Heavenly Father's tender dealings with me, I turned to offer the same wisdom to my son.

WE OBEY FOR LOVE

Repentance, meaning *to change direction*, is required for forgiveness (see Luke 13:3; Acts 3:19; CCC 1861). If I confess and confess but never change direction, I have not accepted his Word; I have not repented. I am not truly sorry. *I have not listened.*

When I could not obey God and quit smoking for any other reason, I finally did it because I wanted to love him more completely. My son obeyed me by changing his direction; he began brushing his teeth without having to be reminded. When he would not obey for any other reason, he finally obeyed me because he loves me.

Likewise, you may be holding a grudge against someone and may not want to forgive that person or treat them with charity because you feel they do not deserve it. If you cannot forgive for love of neighbor, then do it for love of God.

Pope St. John Paul II teaches us that "mystery continually veils itself, covers itself with silence, in order to avoid constructing an idol in place of God."[16] An idol is anything we obey that is not God—a job, a debt, an emotion, an addiction. John Hardon, S.J., notes, "It need not be a figure or representation, and may be a person. In fact, it may be oneself, or some creation of one's own mind or will. An object becomes an idol when it is treated as an end in itself with no reference to God."[17] Our obedience should not be for obedience' sake alone, as though our Father wants to pin us under his divine thumb, as I once imagined. Instead, with Mary, we should strive for obedience out of love.

---

[16] John Paul II, apostolic letter *Orientale Lumen* (May 2, 1995), n. 16, as quoted in Sarah, interview in *Catholic World Report.*

[17] John Hardon, "Idol," in *Modern Catholic Dictionary* (Bardstown, KY: Inter Mirifica, 1999), 264.

OBEDIENCE IS TRUE LISTENING

In addition to merely doing what one is told, scriptural use of the term *obedience* carries emphatic connotations of hearing. Jesus learned *to listen* to God through the things he suffered: "Although he was a Son, he learned obedience through what he suffered; and being made perfect he became the source of eternal salvation to all who obey him" (Hebrews 5:8-9). If this is true of Jesus, how much truer is it for us?

Can we also learn to hear God through our sufferings? Is there some way our sufferings can contribute, through him, to the eternal salvation of those we love and pray for? The Cross offers an emphatic *yes.*

What do I mean?

Praying like Mary with LOVE the Word helped heal me of a profoundly distorted understanding of who God is. I emerged from childhood with what I call a "father wound." Although not physically abusive, my dad was authoritarian, dominating, and controlling, and I was mostly afraid of him. My fear was exacerbated by an intuitive and empathic temperament that made me "feel" his anger in a way that also instilled a profound sense of "badness" and "worthlessness" in me. Because a child's understanding of God is first formed through the relationship (or lack of one) with his or her earthly father, I could not call God "Father" without fear. My relationships with God and with men other than my dad suffered when my father wound provoked a sometimes violent rebellion against authority. My marriage labored under the destruction and "vomit" of the rage and fear I carried.

As soon as I proved myself determined to hear God speak to me through the Scriptures, as soon as I was really *listening*, he used Proverbs 26:11 to point out my "vomit" and called me to obedience: "Has the LORD as great delight in burnt offerings and sacrifices, as in obeying the voice [Word] of the LORD? Behold, to obey is better than sacrifice, and to listen than the fat of rams. For rebellion is as the sin of divination [witchcraft], and stubbornness is as iniquity and idolatry" (1 Samuel 15:22-23). With that one passage he confronted me face-to-Face, but with such gentleness that he did not break the bruised reed of me (see Isaiah 42:3).

Ultimately, prayer in the Scriptures is acceptance of the cleansing of "our hearts of certain false images drawn 'from this world.' ... God our Father transcends the categories of the created world. To impose our own ideas in this area 'upon him' would be to fabricate idols to adore or pull down. To pray to the Father is to enter into his mystery as he is and as the Son has revealed him to us" (CCC 2779). As the *Catechism* says, such false images of him may come from our parents, as in my own case. I was able to accept the truth of his Word and tried valiantly to obey. But my healing and obedience required ongoing, long-term availability and discipline in the Scriptures, and patience under the suffering I experienced in the meantime. Like Jesus, I learned to listen through what I suffered (see again Hebrews 5:8-9).

Without daily discipline in the Scriptures, our work, family, and responsibilities become distractions and impediments to listening, sometimes painfully so. Rather than facilitating our listening, they can prevent the effectiveness of our prayer (see Matthew 13:1-23). When we carefully cultivate a daily practice of listening with Mary in the Word, those "distractions" and sufferings become what I call "pop quizzes"—they are transformed into opportunities to practice what we listened to God say to us in the Scriptures that morning or that week. We are able to interact with the people we connect with on a daily basis in a spirit of charity and even awe, as we discover how God is using them to help us heal and grow.

LET'S REVIEW

Let's review how to listen like Mary.

- *Mary is the "mother of listening"* because she knows how to listen to God and interpret his Word to her.

- *Listening requires a daily discipline* of silence and solitude.

- *Silence is both outer and inner.*

- *It will take forty days* to give birth to a new habit of praying like Mary.

- *Praying in the Scriptures is a face-to-Face encounter* with God.

- *If I love God, I obey* him.

- *Listening = obedience.*

INVITATION

The word *disciple* means "learner"; it's where we get the word *discipline*. Mary shows us that true discipleship is more than a hit-or-miss practice. Rather, it is a daily, continuing *discipline* of abiding, accompanying, or living in and with Christ, the Word. Let us pray.

GOD PROMPT
Practice LOVE the Word®

L–Listen (*Receive the Word.*)

"If you continue in my word, you are truly my disciples" (John 8:31).

O–Observe (*Place yourself in the narrative, imagining every detail.*)

One way to "continue in" God's Word is to memorize it. Spend some time memorizing this verse so that it finds a home in you.

Using all your senses, imagine the Scriptures as a home in which Jesus lives and beckons you to stay with him. With what manner of hospitality does he welcome you? What does it smell like? What do you hear? Taste? Feel? What do you talk about together?

Read the verse several times, emphasizing each Word in turn, like this:

"**If** you continue in my word, you are truly my disciples" (John 8:31).

"If **you** continue in my word, you are truly my disciples" (John 8:31).

"If you **continue** in my word, you are truly my disciples" (John 8:31).

"If you continue **in** my word, you are truly my disciples" (John 8:31).

"If you continue in **my** word, you are truly my disciples" (John 8:31).

After you have emphasized each word of the verse, return to the L–listen section and read the verse again. Where do you sense this verse is speaking about the events of your own life? What is God saying to you through this verse?

What does it mean to you to be a disciple of Christ? What does Jesus say it means, then, to be his disciple?

V–Verbalize *(Pray about your thoughts and emotions.)*

Remembering that he loves you and that you are in his presence, talk to God about the particulars of your O–*observe* step.

E–Entrust *(May it be done to me according to your Word!)*

Thank you, Lord, that we can abide in your Word, that you make it a home for us. What a comforting thought. May your Word be at home in us every day from this day forward. Amen +

Chapter Three

Step 2: O–Observe

Probably the most frequent question I receive in my travels and interactions is, "How do I know when I am hearing God's voice, and when I am pulling out words and phrases to suit my purposes?"

How do we know?

The first principle must always be, does it line up with Church teaching? Because the Holy Spirit speaks primarily through the Church: "The Holy Fathers, we say, are of supreme authority, whenever they all interpret in one and the same manner any text of the Bible, as pertaining to the doctrine of faith or morals; for their unanimity clearly evinces that such interpretation has come down from the Apostles as a matter of Catholic faith."[1]

But our faith is not in the Fathers, brilliant as they are. As John Henry Cardinal Newman observes, "We receive those doctrines which they thus teach, not merely because they teach them, but because they bear witness that all Christians everywhere then held them."[2]

---

[1] Leo XIII, *Providentissimus Deus* (November 18, 1893), 39, from vatican.va/.

[2] John Henry Newman, "The Patristical Idea of Antichrist," lecture 1, in *Discussions and Arguments on Various Subjects* (London: Longman, Green, 1907), 45, available at newmanreader.org/.

Beyond lining up with Church teaching, however, we know we are hearing from God when what we hear is confirmed in observation—by seeing what we read and what God presses upon our hearts fall directly in line with the issues in our lives.

Mary embraces the Word in more than a cerebral way that does not penetrate or move her. She knows how to listen and ponder God's Word in her heart. But isn't listening only part of hearing God? Don't we also need to know what the Word *means* and what God wants us to do with it?

Understanding how the Word applies to us is the second step of LOVE the Word. Mary plunges with God beneath the superficial reality of verbal expression to its meaning. Like Mary, we interpret the Word we have heard by *observing* our relationships and circumstances.

Going beyond contemplation, Mary takes those thoughts out into the world, where she interprets what she has heard through the events of her life. She *observes.* When she visits her kinswoman Elizabeth, who is pregnant in old age, Mary observes God's Word in action. Mary knows—as she sees the reality of God at work in Elizabeth and within herself in the miracle of carrying Jesus—that nothing will be impossible with God.

Pope Francis points out that Mary observes the Word precisely *because* she ponders and interprets it through the events and people in her life:

> This is also true in our life: listening to God who speaks to us, and listening also to daily reality, paying attention to people, to events, because the Lord is at the door of our life and knocks in many ways, he puts signs on our path;

he gives us the ability to see them. Mary is the mother of listening, of attentive listening to God and of equally attentive listening to the events of life.[3]

To Mary, daily reality and the events of life constitute the *meaning* of God's Word to her. She shows us that our own relationships and circumstances contain the meaning of God's daily Word to each of us individually.

Another word for "observe" is *meditate*. Do we read God's Word and hear it every day with a heart that searches for him in our relationships and circumstances, or are we just pushing through it to check it off our list? Remembering that we are in the presence of the Holy Spirit, we observe the events and people in our lives with him. Where does the Word that I read this morning connect with my circumstances, relationships, and habits today? Do we obey that Word when we observe its perspective on our lives?

OBSERVE YOUR PATTERNS

In chapter 1, I shared my first shocking encounter with God in his Word from Proverbs 26:11: *"Like a dog that returns to his vomit is a fool who repeats his folly."*

Once you have listened to and heard God's Word, how do you discern what it *means* for you? Pope Francis says Mary interpreted the Word she received by observing the events and relationships in her life. I found this to be true for me as well, as Mary's model for how to observe the Word.

In my case, the pattern of "vomit" in my life was so obvious I could barely miss it, because there was destruction

---

[3]   Francis, "Recital of the Holy Rosary," n. 1.

everywhere in its wake. In order to begin healing the destruction, God addressed the profound wound beneath. He used his Word to point out the reality that (1) my vomit was part of a pattern, and (2) it was a disgusting reaction to the pattern. Then he gave me an opportunity to practice. I call such opportunities "pop quizzes" now.

God will begin healing your destruction and wounds, too, as you observe your own circumstances and events through his Word on a daily basis. Here's what I mean; this was one of my very first "pop quizzes."

I sent a wedding invitation to my dad, and he called to summon me for an emergency discussion. I knew it was a futile errand: no one "discussed" things with my dad. He told you what to do, and you did it. End of "discussion." But I went anyway because I knew better than to refuse.

As I anticipated, he demanded that I move the wedding date. He said it was too soon, and that I was too young. Only twenty years old, I probably was too young, but I had also been out on my own from the age of seventeen; I had my own apartment and worked a full-time job while attending school full time on scholarship. I supported myself and was independent. I felt ready. I was also tired of being intimidated and controlled by my authoritarian father, whom I saw irregularly after he and my mother divorced following my thirteenth birthday.

But even more than that, I was afraid of God. The Bible says fornication is a sin, and sin will send you to hell. My future husband and I were living together, a situation I wanted to remedy as soon as possible. I told my father I was not moving the wedding date. The "discussion" got heated, and I am not proud of flipping him a bird as I left angry. My father chased me out the door and down the driveway, yelling, "You'd better be sure this is what you want. You'd better be *sure* this is what you want!"

He did not attend my wedding. He did not walk me down the aisle. He did not celebrate my marriage. We did not speak for several years. And then ...

I came home from work and noticed the mail stacked on the kitchen table. A pink birthday card rested there, addressed to me in my father's all-capitals handwriting. My heart pounded as I picked it up to read it, and then I exploded in rage, as uncontrollably as "vomiting" all over my husband, when I realized he had opened and already read the first words my father had offered *me* in three years. I was *angry*.

My explosive anger was not confined to this instance—I had a history of angry outbursts—but that birthday was the first, and thankfully the only, time I ever experienced blackout rage. When my rage was exhausted, I collapsed in tears of pain and shame at my inexcusable behavior. I was terrified at the realization I could not remember most of what I had done and said. I remember asking God, "What in the world is *wrong* with me?"

God answered me the very next morning in Scripture.

As I mentioned earlier, I was twenty-six days into reading one chapter of Proverbs every day for my quiet time in the Scriptures. That was the day I discovered my "vomit" in Proverbs 26:11, in a pithy and even surprisingly humorous answer to my embarrassed question about my unreasonable behavior: "Like a dog that returns to his vomit is a fool who repeats his folly."

I call my experience in the Scriptures that morning a pop quiz now, because after some practice, I realized my circumstances always correspond somehow to what I receive from God in the Scriptures. He speaks to me regularly in his Word about patterns and their roots in my behavior, relationships, and circumstances, especially those that are most painful. As C. S. Lewis pointed out, God shouts in our pains. Pain is God's "megaphone to rouse a deaf world."[4]

That proverb only began my journey. I recognized my glaring sin but still felt a lack of full responsibility. When my rage erupted, I had no idea where it came from, and I felt it was out of my control. In my mind that meant that my rage was not completely my responsibility. I justified my outbursts as simply due to a passionate personality, saying, "Everyone would be perfectly fine if they just didn't make me mad!" and "I can't help it, Lord!"

S-T-O-P THE VOMIT

Within the week, he answered me with this: "Be angry, but sin not; commune with your own hearts on your beds, and be silent. Offer right sacrifices, and put your trust in the LORD" (Psalm 4:4-5). At the time, I had no idea anyone, ever, could be angry without sinning. I didn't even know such a thing was possible. Now, I teach what I learned.

S-T-O-P is a tool for "vomit control":

---

4   C. S. Lewis, *The Problem of Pain* (San Francisco, CA: HarperOne, 2003), 91.

STOP!

Sᴉɴ ɴᴏᴛ,

Tᴇʟʟ Gᴏᴅ,

Oꜰꜰᴇʀ ᴛʜᴇ ʀɪɢʜᴛ sᴀᴄʀɪꜰɪᴄᴇ, ᴀɴᴅ

Pᴜᴛ ʏᴏᴜʀ ᴛʀᴜsᴛ ɪɴ Gᴏᴅ.

I *can* be angry without sin. In fact, St. Thomas Aquinas quotes a scholar who says, "He who is not angry, whereas he has cause to be, sins. For unreasonable patience is the hotbed of many vices; it fosters negligence and incites ... even the good to wrong."[5] So anger, as an emotion given to me in the image of my Creator, is not wrong. Instead, my actions when I am angry are the issue.

Psalm 4:4-5 tells me I can control my angry behavior. God used that Scripture and Proverbs 26:11 to confront me about my behavior pattern of rage. Not anger: rage. And then he began offering me pop quizzes so I could observe and put into practice what he was teaching me through his Word.

At the root of my anger was a fear of criticism stemming from my father wound. No matter how high my performance when I was growing up, it was the existing defect that was often pointed out. I became both a perfectionist and obsessive-compulsive to avoid all criticism. I suffered from self-condemnation.

If you too are suffering from such woes of life, be at peace. God's heart is heavy over the great destruction that overwhelms us through our wounds: our behavior suffers,

---

[5] Thomas Aquinas, *Summa Theologica* II-II.158.8, available at newadvent.org /summa/. In the *Summa*, the quotation is inaccurately attributed to St. John Chrysostom.

our relationships suffer, we self-medicate. We get into sin-ruts and do not know where they come from, when mostly they come from these wounds. God's word reveals his heart: "Let my eyes run down with tears night and day, and let them not cease, for the virgin daughter of my people is struck down with a great wound, with a very grievous blow" (Jeremiah 14:17). That is us. We are the people of God. After Mary, who is the Sign of the Church, we are the virgin daughter of God's people. He says we have an incurable wound. Incurable for us, but praise and thanks be to God, it is not incurable for him. God's Word is new every morning.

As soon as I was willing to take a hard look at my behavior and its roots, God began dealing with my hurt and anger through my daily Scripture reading. Simultaneously, I began to realize that my anger was most often triggered by my husband's "gift of criticism." Wounds from his own childhood exacerbate his naturally precise temperament. He actually has the same gift of righteousness that Moses had, as the great Bringer of the Law. But when it is out of balance, this gift of righteousness is a destructive, critical defense mechanism. My husband offered me his gift of criticism, and I could not bear it. Early in our marriage I lashed out in pain and anger.

Psalm 4:4-5 taught me not to act out aggressively when provoked, but then I went to the other extreme: I stuffed my anger by pretending I was not angry; I developed problems with passive-aggression and depression, which psychologists tell us is repressed anger.

God's quiet, persistent guidance taught me self-control and proper expression of anger (Sin not). I was invited to talk to him, and only him, when I was hurt or angry (Tell

God). We would decide together the best course of action, the "right sacrifices" outlined in Psalm 4:5 (Offer the right sacrifice). Usually my right sacrifice was to grow up in charity. But occasionally I had to erect boundaries with others. Either way, I had to trust him with the consequences of the sacrifice I made in obedience (Put your trust in God). God taught me to S-T-O-P the "vomit."

As I observed with him over time, the Lord pointed out the underlying pattern in my anger: my rage erupted when I was criticized by men who were in positions of authority over me, especially those with aggressive or critical leadership styles, especially those I respected or loved. I knew God expected me to change this generational sin-pattern through his grace, and I found he was more than happy to help me do it through Scripture and meditation when I sought him in his Word through my LOVE the Word practice and examined my life through the pop quizzes that triggered my "vomit."

Along with counseling, mentorship, books, and spiritual reading, God pointed out how those episodes stemmed from particularly painful memories. In his presence and with his help, I poured out the hurt and anger I had buried in those painful memories, the real injustice of the things done to me, and he healed them.

Today, I no longer have a rage problem.

Not everyone battles rage. You probably have a different "vomit." But you have a go-to sin that is out-of-control, one that you "vomit" whenever events occur that provoke particular memories. As you observe God's Word with Mary on a daily basis, S-T-O-P will work for your vomit, too.

Ultimately, I found the answer to *How do I know I am hearing God?* to be *He makes me know through Scripture*. Over the long term, the answer is, I learn from practice, from hearing and observing a word that comes true, or is true, day after day in pop quizzes and other events.

MARY OBSERVES DAILY REALITY

Pope Emeritus Benedict XVI pointed out that Mary's extraordinary holiness is the result of a deep relationship with God characterized by her ponderings of events with him in the silence of her heart.[6] Under the Word of God, Mary *observes* the landscape of her life and relationships.

> Jesus, too, always observed the circumstances and events in his life.

> Jesus said to them, "Truly, truly, I say to you, the Son can do nothing of his own accord, but only what he sees the Father doing; for whatever he does, that the Son does likewise. For the Father loves the Son, and shows him all that he himself is doing." (John 5:19-20)

When we listen to God's Word every day and *observe* our habits, relationships, and circumstances, we can trust that the Holy Spirit will show us where he is working in our lives to free us from sin patterns, and where he wants our cooperation: "If you continue in my word, you are truly my disciples, and you will know the truth, and the truth will make you free. ... Every one who commits sin is a slave to sin" (John 8:31-32, 8:34). Like Mary's faith, our faith can be infused with the generative power of the Holy Spirit through his Word and be informed by it.

---

6   Benedict XVI, "Without Mary There Is No Church."

We begin observing by discerning our behavior patterns in our relationships and circumstances, through which God has been speaking all along. As our daily LOVE the Word practice speaks to those behavior patterns, difficult relationships, and tangled circumstances, we are empowered and healed day by day, "faith for faith" (Romans 1:17), through the Holy Spirit. We become a witness, a bearer of Jesus into the world. This is what Mary longs to see accomplished in us through our prayer practice.

If we embark on this endeavor with any seriousness and discipline, we begin to discern that God regularly allows the provocation of negative feelings and infliction of our pains in order to pull out our faults and sin by the root, particularly the predominant fault.[7] Hence, the pop quizzes. For "we know that in everything God works for good with those who love him, who are called according to his purpose" (Romans 8:28).

"The wages of sin is death" (Romans 6:23). What dies under my withering rage? What could my unchecked "vomit" really cost me? Ultimately, such passions can lead us to hell. But most of us never consider how destructive sin really is in the day-to-day short term. Sin disconnects us from love. Love dies a slow, painful death. My marriage, my children's emotional and spiritual health, jobs, freedom from certain habits, my salvation and relationship to God, all suffered under the destruction of my rage.

Like Mary, I observe the events of my life in God's presence to find the meaning of his Word to me. God will speak to

---

7   More information on discerning and combating one's predominant fault can be found in my books *Unleashed, How to Receive Everything the Holy Spirit Wants to Give You* (2015) and *Fearless, A Catholic Woman's Guide to Spiritual Warfare* (2016), both from Ave Maria Press.

me about my sin through his Word, and he will confirm that Word through my daily reality and relationships.

HOW TO OBSERVE EVENTS

My oldest son shares a temperament with my husband; both are able to size up a person or situation in no time flat, usually critically.

When our boys were little I often warned my husband about this "gift," and how my father had instilled a wound in me in exactly the same critical way. He took concrete steps to mitigate it, but the Eeyore syndrome—the tendency to see things in the most melancholy light—had been imparted to my husband by his own parents and is as much who he is as breathing. Our recurring fight for the first decade of our marriage was my "over-sensitivity" to his criticism. And because God has spent my entire adulthood working on this wound, I admit it is true that I can make a mountain out of any molehill.

When my oldest son was about seventeen, he began coming home late at night after work in retail and unloading his difficult day on me. I am most depleted at night, so hearing his key in the door brought on an almost-dread, because I knew I was in for a thirty-minute barrage of negativity and criticism that I would be unable to absorb and disperse before bed. I often went to bed angry. I began to feel like a balloon in a cactus patch. I wanted my son to be able to talk to me, but I hated the nightly negativity.

Eventually everything my son said and did began to get on my nerves. The empath in me that "feels" other people's emotions as though they are my own had me on defense against either my son or husband all the time. I was habitually hurt or angry or cringing. Emotionally raw. I finally told my husband, "One of you has to go. I've spent two decades dealing with your gift of criticism; I can't handle two of you." I became openly critical of my son.

The situation came to a head one evening while I was sleeping, when they both came home late and tired. My son popped off a smart-alecky reply to a bit of his father's smart-alecky criticism.

Neither of them can stand a smart aleck.

My husband poked my adult son in the chest and barked in his face about how ungrateful and entitled he is. My son said nothing, but he packed his bags the next morning and left without a word.

He was gone for a week.

Because I had slept through the incident, I didn't hear my son's side of the story before he left, and because I had been dealing with my own irritable reactions toward him for weeks, I automatically took my husband's side. We were both offended at my son's presumption. He needed to learn a lesson, absolutely. Our emotions went through the gamut of anger, then guilt, then sadness, then anger again.

I knew enough to leave off the advice and allow both my husband and son the room to reconcile however they might, so I was patient for several days while praying the readings, through which God propped me up. But I went to him in panicky tears after several days when my son had still not come home and had not communicated with us at all. How could he just leave and remain silent, even after his father had reached out in apology?

The Holy Spirit answered me through the daily readings: "Fathers, do not provoke your children to anger, but bring them up in the discipline and instruction of the Lord" (Ephesians 6:4). This verse talks about fathers, true, but I knew the Holy Spirit was also talking to me. I *was* critical, and maybe my son could say the same thing I had, and "just couldn't handle two of us."

HOW TO OBSERVE RELATIONSHIPS

Jesus said:

> Judge not, that you be not judged. For with the judgment you pronounce you will be judged, and the measure you give will be the measure you get. Why do you see the speck that is in your brother's eye, but do not notice the log that is in your own eye? Or how can you say to your brother, "Let me take the speck out of your eye," when there is the log in your own eye? You hypocrite, first take the log out of your own eye, and then you will see clearly to take the speck out of your brother's eye. (Matthew 7:1-5)

St. Catherine of Siena echoed this message beautifully: "I would have you know that every virtue of yours and every vice is put into action by means of your neighbors. ... For, if [one] does not love Me, she cannot be in charity with her neighbor; and thus, all evils derive from the soul's deprivation of love of Me and her neighbor."[8]

When my son first left our home, I felt somewhat smug that my husband had finally experienced a clear consequence of his criticism through someone besides me. Between them, I

---

8   Catherine of Sienna, *The Dialogue* (Mahwah, NJ: Paulist Press, 1980), 33, 38.

thought sarcastically, there should never be a need for a Final Judgment, because the two of them will have it all wrapped up.

"*They* have issues with criticism," I said, and yet the reading pointed out that I'd also been contributing to the breakdown in our relationship all along. My son's negativity repetitively tweaked my father wound, and I automatically fell into criticism myself as a defense mechanism. In pointing out the speck of their shared critical spirit, I neglected to see the log in my own eye.

During my prayer with the Word that morning I was heartbroken. I was truly repentant. Providentially, my husband also read that same passage—"Fathers, do not provoke your children to anger" (Ephesians 6:4)—and was apologetic as well. We were finally ready to have a constructive conversation with our son about responsibility, his *and* ours.

This is what family is meant to be: a place to learn from one another in the safety of our love for each other. Our work environments, parish families, and the larger Church are all places and relationships of formation. God is always speaking to us through other people, whether we like them or not. People who trigger our negative emotions are especially revealing, as they reflect us to ourselves like emotional and spiritual mirrors—especially the sides of ourselves that we subconsciously deem abhorrent, the aspects of ourselves or the desires that we repress and deny.

There is never a moment when God does not approach us in the mediation of another person. My neighbor is my teacher. Whatever offensive faults I discern in my neighbor simply point to my own self-righteousness in denied or hidden faults or desires, often multiplied several times over, as a log is to a speck. Like Mary, as we *observe* our relationships in the light of the daily readings, we discern the meaning of the Word for us there.

As Jesus pointed out, we tend to draw attention to the faults of others in order to cover our own, but in doing so we disown a shadowy part of ourselves that we find painful or unattractive. St. Paul sheds some light on this subject in his discourse on the body of Christ, of which each of us is part:

> God arranged the organs in the body, each one of them, as he chose. If all were a single organ, where would the body be? As it is, there are many parts, yet one body. The eye cannot say to the hand, "I have no need of you," nor again the head to the feet, "I have no need of you." On the contrary, the parts of the body which seem to be weaker are indispensable. ... Now you are the body of Christ and individually members of it. (1 Corinthians 12:18–22, 27)

My attitude toward my son told him I had no need of him, but my reaction to the variations in our personalities and temperaments had more to do with my father wound than with him. In fact, I would go so far as to say that God offers our relationships expressly to help teach us the lessons we need to learn about ourselves. I believe he gave me a husband and son with similar temperaments specifically to weed out my father wound. Vestiges of that wound came to light through my son after I learned to deal with criticism from my husband and others. The Holy Spirit gives talents, temperaments, personalities, gifts, and strengths. The Holy Spirit was using my son to show me my own critical spirit. How, then, can we say we have no need of others' differences?

The Bible says condemnation of another person can make me guilty of their sin as well (Matthew 7:1-5; Galatians 6:1).

Additionally, we must resist the temptation to believe God is speaking to us for someone else's benefit. We may read a passage and think, *Boy, So-and-so really needs to hear this*, and hurry to share what God has told us about "them." But when God speaks *to* me, he is speaking about *me*. I must resist focusing on the speck in another's eye and always search for the log in my own.

Recently, my husband came to me troubled that God had been warning him through the readings over a period of weeks about possible trouble in our marriage, or an attack on it. We read the same readings each day, and naturally, since he is the head of our household, I worried at first that he might be right. My husband talked to me about his concerns several times over those weeks, insisting on the consistency of what he was hearing. But I was not hearing what he was hearing in the Scriptures, a fact that he said made him feel "hopeless." We share the same Holy Spirit, so we were both troubled and confused. I was not guilty of any sin whatsoever against our marriage, and was not even experiencing temptation along that line, yet he continued to imply I must be, somehow. Was one of us not "hearing" correctly? Was one of us in denial? We both grew frustrated with each other.

Over time, I began to suspect exactly what my husband was indeed hearing: he, personally, was under spiritual attack, and it was affecting our marriage. But he was looking outwardly at me rather than inwardly at himself. Thanks be to God, I know the Scriptures, so the long-term fear and discouragement he was experiencing were red flags to me, "for God did not give us a spirit of timidity" (2 Timothy 1:7, rendered "fear" in other translations); St. Ignatius of Loyola also teaches in his discernment of spirits that discouragement is never from God, because it clouds faith and hope. Our mutual confusion was another red flag, because God is not a "God of confusion but of peace" (1 Corinthians 14:33). I spoke to my husband about the principle, *When God speaks to you, he speaks about you.* I ran to Our Lady and St. Joseph, Terror of Demons, who is also my husband's patron saint, and prayed for a breakthrough. Then I shared my suspicions and the legitimate reasons for them.

Providentially, I came home from a speaking event armed with a book that specifically addressed his experiences. We indeed experienced a breakthrough, and learned a valuable lesson in self-knowledge: When God speaks to you, he speaks about *you.*

When we look outwardly to other people in accusation, we must be aware of the influence of Satan, the "accuser" (Revelation 12:10). We may see another's sin, and even have to correct that person, but we must resist condemnation, pray for them (see 1 John 5:16), and look for the self-knowledge God wants to share with us through them. The measure of judgment or forgiveness we offer them will be the measure we receive ourselves (see Luke 6:37–38).

When we practice this biblical mandate, those who seem to be enemies become agents of holiness. By observing our relationships through the Word on a daily basis, even the most difficult ones, they become opportunities for charity and humility, opportunities for a purer faith, opportunities for restoration and renewal.

Because our relationships with God and other people are built on our own and others' personalities and temperaments, it is also helpful to also know something about those.

FIAT: HOW PERSONALITIES AND TEMPERAMENTS AFFECT OBSERVING

Fiat is the Latin term we use for Mary's response to God's Word, "May it be done." Literally, *fiat* means "to make" or "to do" or "to let." Interestingly, in the Latin translation of the Bible, the Creation account in Genesis uses the same word, something like "God said *fiat*, and light was made," or "God said: *Be* light *made*. And light was made" (Genesis 1:3). As already noted, Creation and re-creation both began with God's Word. God's fiat was creation; Mary's fiat was consent to the Incarnation in her of the Son who would renew all of creation.

In their book *Prayer and Temperament*, Chester Michael and Marie Norrisey offer different prayer forms for diverse personality types according to the Myers-Briggs Type Indicator and the shorter Keirsey Temperament Sorter. Their classifications can provide guidance in formulating our own particular ways to offer a fiat, our own yes.

Through their Prayer Project, which is based on these personality indicators, Michael and Norrisey have developed a different approach to prayer and spirituality for each of the four basic temperaments. They present these spirituality approaches as Ignatian, Augustinian, Franciscan, and Thomistic, but re-ordered, the first letter of each spells a handy acronym: *FIAT!*

For me, one of the most interesting findings in their research was the confirmation of something the Church has inherently operated under for hundreds of years: The Franciscan, Ignatian, Augustinian, and Thomistic (FIAT) forms of spirituality and prayer are *all* applied in *lectio divina*—as they are in LOVE the Word, too. According to Michael and Norrisey, *L–listening* uses the *senses* (Ignatian), either in reading or hearing; *O–observing* uses the intellect's *thinking* (Thomistic) function to reflect and ruminate on the Word received; *V–verbalizing* uses the *feeling* (Franciscan) function to communicate with God; and *E–entrusting* employs *intuition* (Augustinian) to integrate or unite the prayer experience. "This ancient type of prayer has been used by Christians more often than any other method of prayer. This is understandable since it employs all four psychological functions and therefore is an ideal form of prayer for all the different types and temperaments of personality."[9]

Using such classifications may sound like we're overthinking prayer, but different personality types process information differently. Some personality indicators are so accurate and insightful, corporations use them to help employees maximize productivity and healthy working relationships, universities use them to pair roommates, and therapists use them to help patients unravel and improve difficult relationships. As one who has taken such tests, I've found that understanding my own personality and temperament and familiarizing myself with the others eliminates an overwhelming majority of misunderstandings and conflicts that would have surely occurred without such knowledge. The ability to discern that interpersonal conflicts are due to simple personality differences rather than malice makes one a proficient peacemaker!

---

9   Chester Michael and Marie Norrisey, *Prayer and Temperament* (Charlottesville, VA: The Open Door, 1991), 25.

While the O-observe step is basically Thomistic, I have adapted it to follow each of the FIAT approaches, as you will experience in the God Prompts at the end of this and the following chapters. Choose whichever style suits you and your temperament. However, I suggest trying all four so you can effectively choose which one to practice on a regular basis.[10] We are each drawn to and proficient in one approach over others, but Michael and Norrisey encourage occasional attempts at those that require more effort, because they engage the subconscious and can reveal otherwise untapped spiritual riches.

By deciphering your personality type to find your best personal approach to the O–observe step, and using that as a guideline in approaching the daily readings of the Church, you will find that LOVE the Word as a prayer method will speak to every stage of your development, whether you are a beginner or advanced, and to every personality and temperament.

In summary, God speaks to me every day through the daily Scripture readings about the events of my life and the people I encounter. Mary shows me that observing them in his presence on a daily basis is the key to the healing, freedom, and the abundant life I am looking for and that the Holy Spirit wants to accomplish in my life. In his presence, we L–listen and O–observe. Next we will V–verbalize.

---

[10]   For more practice with FIAT, see Sonja's weekly radio show and podcast, *The Bible Study Evangelista Show*, at biblestudyevangelista.com. The show notes for each episode include a LOVE the Word devotion according to FIAT, along with the audio teaching.

LET'S REVIEW

Let's review how to observe our relationships and circumstances in order to understand God's Word to us.

- *The Holy Spirit is always speaking* through his Word to address my circumstances and relationships.

- *Circumstances and relationships often grow more and more painful* the longer I fail to hear the message in them.

- *Every human being experiences terrible pain* and problems, but suffering can contribute to my salvation.

- *I can learn to hear God through my suffering* if I can submit to painful circumstances the way Jesus did.

- *If I experience something twice or more, I should pay attention* and discern the pattern.

- *When God speaks to me, he speaks about me.*

- *If I am not sure I am hearing him, I should wait* to see if he confirms it, especially through pop quizzes and the Scriptures.

INVITATION

While Mary gives us the model to strive for as we pray and reflect on passages through LOVE the Word, the average human reality is largely imperfection and disobedience. Therefore, we should study how God works when we are not obedient or are unwilling to offer God a full fiat. To that end, Jonah is a realistic study example, because when Jonah hears the Word of God, he does the exact opposite of what he is told. How does God work when we say no to what we have heard, whether it is because we are inexperienced, timid, suspicious, or flat-out rebellious? Jonah considered Nineveh his enemy. What does the passage say about how we should treat our enemies?

GOD PROMPT
Practice LOVE the Word®

L–Listen (*Receive the Word.*)

"Now the word of the LORD came to Jonah the son of Amittai, saying, 'Arise, go to Nineveh, that great city, and cry against it; for their wickedness has come up before me.' But Jonah rose to flee to Tarshish from the presence of the LORD" (Jonah 1:1–3).

O–Observe (*Connect the passage to recent events.*)

F | Franciscan

Think of someone who has hurt you, or someone you dislike or consider your enemy. Make a list of all the good, positive things you can find in that person. How can you foster these good qualities in this person? Spend some time praying for him or her.

I | Ignatian

As you re-read Jonah 1:1-3 in the *L–listen* step, above, put yourself in Jonah's place and imagine the scenario. Where are you when the Word of the Lord comes to you? How do you know it is him? Does he speak audibly or silently? Does he swoop in beside you?

Is the air charged with electricity? How do you feel when he calls you to share your faith with your enemy? What happens when you ignore God's Word and instead book a trip to Siberia? What do you think will happen to you next? What about the people to whom you were called? Why do you run away from God's command?

A | Augustinian

Think of someone who has hurt you, or someone whom you dislike or consider your enemy. How is God calling you through this passage to share your faith with this person?

T | Thomistic

Search online or in *The Great Adventure Bible* for Jonah's location on a Bible map. What do the locations of Nineveh and Tarshish tell you about Jonah? About God?

V–Verbalize (*Pray about your thoughts and emotions.*)

In guilt, "I called to the LORD, out of my distress, and he answered me" (Jonah 2:2). In rebellion, "I called to the LORD, out of my distress, and he answered me." In impossible circumstances, "I called to the LORD, out of my distress, and he answered me." In spite of my painful consequences, "I called to the LORD, out of my distress, and he answered me."

E–Entrust (*May it be done to me according to your Word!*)

Perhaps you'd like to wonder at and cherish, now, God's never-ending pursuit of your loyal love, even in the midst of your disobedience.

Chapter Four

Step 3: V–Verbalize

When our "mother of listening" received the Word from God in prayer, she hugged the secret close. When she realized that Elizabeth knew and understood her miracle, Mary *verbalized* back to God her understanding of that Word in Elizabeth's presence, and they rejoiced together. The Word of God that Mary listened to and observed erupted from her heart in verbal expression. To this day, her Magnificat remains in Scripture and is sung every day in the Liturgy of the Hours as the evening prayer-song of the Church.

HOW KING DAVID VERBALIZED

We already know that Mary was familiar with another biblical model for verbalizing prayer in the psalms. The psalms (meaning *songs*) of the Old Testament are King David's "prayer journal" of poetic song-prayers, which we use to instruct, edify, and guide our own prayer and verbalization today. Both the Magnificat and the psalms are perfect examples of how we can and should *verbalize* our thoughts and prayers about what God says to us in the Scriptures.

A gifted musician and song writer, David's transparent psalms follow the ups and downs of his formation and his kingdom and even speak prophetically of Jesus as the fulfillment of David's kingly, priestly, and prophetic reign.

David, meaning "beloved," was the youngest of Jesse's sons and shepherd of the family's flocks, the last and the least likely to be chosen for anything special. Yet God called David a man after his own heart (see 1 Samuel 13:14; Acts 13:22), perhaps because he was uniquely sensitive and submissive to the Holy Spirit. I find that a fascinating thought. Very Marian.

King Saul, the first Israelite king, was rejected for failing to regard his position as one through which God himself ruled his own people. Saul had behaved as an individualist, presumptuously, and in ways that did not reflect God's authority. He was not a man who followed God's own heart, and God replaced him with David. God chose David the shepherd boy, and David was anointed king of Israel at about fifteen years of age. But David did not ascend to the throne until after an extended time of formation, under God's hand, while Saul continued to reign as the first King of Israel.

A WARRIOR AND A POET

Scriptural accounts of David's manly vigor make him sound almost like a legend, but it is known from archaeological excavations that he was a real person, a real king. As a youth, he killed lion and bear with his bare hands to protect the sheep in his care (see 1 Samuel 17:34-36). At the age of fifteen or so, David was the only Israelite in the whole nation, including even King Saul, who would confront the Philistine giant who had mocked the Israelites and their God for forty days (see 1 Samuel 17). Although he was too small to even walk in King Saul's armor, David had already far surpassed him in stature. He slew the giant and won an entire war for the Israelites in one fell swoop by cutting off Goliath's head in the name of the Lord.

The ladies in the kingdom loved him. Saul's children loved him: Jonathan the prince was his best friend; Michal the princess became his wife. Saul's soldiers loved him, the most elite calling themselves "David's Mighty Men." While David submitted patiently to God's authority, timing, and provision, God prepared the entire kingdom to accept the leadership of their new king.

Because of his military and physical prowess, David led the Israelite armies in combat, and his successes elevated him to prominence before the men of Saul's kingdom and all the people. But he was no mere powerhouse. Young David's musical sensitivity and talent were regularly employed by King Saul as David played for him at court, and his delicate poetry graces the psalms.

AFTER GOD'S OWN HEART

Fourteen of the psalms were written at specific times in David's life. One of those times is described in 1 Samuel 19:18, when David fled after one of Saul's many jealous attempts to kill him after he killed Goliath. If David killed Goliath and all his "ten thousands," as the women sang (1 Samuel 18:7), I doubt he was afraid of Saul. Rather, David's prayer journal reveals that he submitted to his earthly king while waiting for his heavenly King to elevate him to the throne for which he had already been legitimately anointed.

Fifteen years passed between David's anointing and his actual ascension to the throne. David's years of purification were part of the process required to actually prepare him for the type of leadership and throne to which he was called. During that time, God's *beloved* David was being challenged and confirmed in heroic leadership, because in order to lead heroically, he had to know how to follow heroically. God's call for David was only fulfilled in David's life after many years of extreme, difficult, painful formation.

Finally, in a battle that broke David's heart, God allowed both the king and the prince to be slain, to clear the path for his uncontested reign. David's submissiveness to authority, under God, was affirmed and defended before the whole people.

Although we may often wish things were different, and we could legitimately rebel by word or deed against authorities we disagree with, it simply is not so. Among others throughout the Bible, David's witness proves that authority is of the Lord. Even authority we consider "bad" is an instrument of God (Romans 13:1-2); David inherently knew that to go against Saul as the legitimate king was to align himself against God, under whose authority all things proceed (see 1 Samuel 24:6-7). In submitting so heroically to God's timing and provision, David demonstrated his worthiness to rule on God's behalf.

GOD'S WORD IS THE KEY TO OUR PURPOSE

David reigned for forty years, and the key to his successful reign was his relationship with the Lord, with whom he stayed in constant verbal contact. He continually inquired of

God for his will and permission to act. David demonstrated the importance of his religious convictions to all of Israel very early in and throughout his reign. When he told the Lord he wanted to build the Lord a "house," the Lord replied that, instead, *he* would build David a house. This term, *house*, means a royal dynasty and eternal throne. Surely, when David was first called to be king at the age of fifteen, he could have never imagined that God's intent and purpose for him all along was to create an *eternal* dynasty fulfilled in the Messiah, and that his long, difficult formation period would ready him for such a role in salvation history.

God followed the same pattern of long-term, back-and-forth formation-through-conversation with Adam, Noah, Abraham, and Moses—with all his servants, every biblical person who had a relationship with him and a role in salvation history. What if the same could be true of you somehow? What if your constant contact with God in his Word is the key to knowing and growing into *your* unique purpose? What if it's as simple as hearing in his Word every day how to deal with *your* duties and station in life in ways that make your service to him last into eternity?

David won the everlasting love of God's people, and indeed of all people on earth, not merely as a great warrior or mighty king but as the author of the book of Psalms, some of the most instructive, vulnerable, and tender wisdom literature and poetry of Judaism and Christianity. Unlike other kings, David rose before the sun to pray and chant psalms of praise to God, the King of all kings (see Psalm 59:16, 92:1-3, 143:8). He was not afraid to pour out his heart to God, first as a youth while watching the flocks of sheep in his care, and then as a man who ruled God's family with

God's own spirit and love. The psalms show us David's sincerest and purest trust in God alone, and God honored David in part by preserving them for us in Scripture as prayers of lament, thanksgiving, praise, and prophecy.

According to tradition, the psalms are largely by and about David. Of the psalms he did not write, David appointed most of the other named authors. Without compromising his masculinity one degree, he worshipped and wrote with great tenderness and emotion, sometimes weeping and wailing, then praising with exuberant enthusiasm and joy. Sickness, sin, and gathering enemies were all subjects of his prayers.

Because we have his prayer journal as a record of his thoughts and emotions throughout his life, we can see into David's heart very clearly, especially in the difficult times he experienced. He was so in tune with God's heart that many of his psalms were prophetic of Christ, who quoted David's songs many times, even at his most significant moment on earth, when he cried, "My God, my God, why have you forsaken me?" (Psalm 22:1). Sometimes David's writing lapsed into the very voice and Words of God himself.[1]

As already noted, the ancient psalms occupy a prominent place in the prayers of the Church. They are called the "masterwork" of the Old Testament and of prayer. Indeed, in the history of David—his exile, persecution, struggles, and eventual triumph—the Israelites, collectively and individually, found an expression and prophecy of their own lives, as we do today. No wonder the book of Psalms has served as a boundless source of inspiration, courage,

---

[1]   "Because he clings to me in love, I will deliver him; I will protect him, because he knows my name. When he calls to me, I will answer him; I will be with him in trouble, I will rescue him and honor him. With long life I will satisfy him, and show him my salvation" (Psalm 91:14-16).

and hope throughout the ages of God's people—and to think they are the fruit of the *V–verbalize* step of prayer.

Composed by divine inspiration (we know this because they are included in Sacred Scripture, as is Mary's Magnificat), the Psalms are the most popular poetry collection ever published in world history. Used in the Catholic Church and other Christian churches in daily worship and prayer, the Psalms are the only part of the Bible read at every single Mass. They are a cherished and comprehensive primer on how to *verbalize*.

WHAT TO WRITE

As David listened to God's Word through the prophet Samuel and Mary listened to the angel, we *listen* to the Word of God at Mass, in the Liturgy of the Hours, or in a homily, a Bible teaching, or the Rosary, and we *observe* how God is using his Word to address our circumstances, issues, and relationships. Then it is important to *verbalize* back to God what we believe he has said to us.

David's verbalization typically began with what some have called a "mind dump." In the first lines, he almost always expressed and expelled deep emotion of one type or another directly to God. God taught me this principle, too, when instructing me on how to S-T-O-P from David's Psalm 4:4-5.

Then, before David despaired completely, he would purposely remember times past when God delivered him, and he verbalized his enduring confidence that God would do so again. This review of God's past provision is a major reason why it is important to journal our prayers: later we can look back over the many times God rescued us previously.

David often confessed sin at this point. Then he promised to praise God when God forgave and saved him, or he praised God for his forgiveness, salvation, and provision *before* God acted on his behalf.

Elijah is another example of God's will that we *verbalize* back to him our interpretation of his Word to us, our thoughts and emotions about our circumstances and relationships. God prompted Elijah to pour out his heart twice (1 Kings 19:9, 19:13), when it seemed once was not enough to dispel the strength of his emotion and correct his misperception of his circumstances.

Mary also followed David's pattern, taking time to observe and ponder God's Word before expressing her thoughts and emotions. We can easily imagine Mary pondering God's Word from the angel throughout her six-day walk into the hill country of Judea, and expressing her brimming heart in the Magnificat when Elizabeth revealed her miraculous understanding of Mary's call and role in salvation history.

HOW TO VERBALIZE

Although Mary didn't leave behind a journal of her thoughts and prayers that we know of, consider recording your prayers as David did. Pick out a new journal, touch the empty pages, and anticipate all that might occur in your life and be recorded there. Special journals are not necessary. A seventy-nine-cent spiral notepad or notebook surely suffices as long as you are satisfied with it and will look forward to verbalizing your thoughts and conversations with God. As we saw in David's example, one of the main gifts of journaling is being able to read back over a period of days or weeks and discern the longer arc of God's voice and movement in our lives.

Processing prayer in writing and song is a traditional practice. Saints John of the Cross, Faustina, Elisabeth Leseur, Teresa of Avila, and Thérèse of Lisieux, among many others, male and female, kept prayer journals that continue to provide instruction to the Church on the life of holiness.

In imitating these holy examples, we are not doing creative writing, although our verbal prayers can surely lead to that. Rather, we are free-writing whatever comes into our heads after reading the daily readings and meditating on them in God's presence. We don't edit; we don't worry about grammar, spelling, or style; and we don't stop writing until everything in our hearts and heads is said.

The V—verbalize step is important and even necessary for several reasons. Psychologists tell us that verbal processing—writing down our thoughts and dreams and fears—is therapeutic in itself, powerful enough to effect change, boost immunity, and assist in healing wounds, trauma, and anxiety.[2] It is not even necessary to reread your writings to derive healing benefits, but only to search for meaning in your experiences through your writing, so don't worry about what you write. Concentrate instead on just doing it, writing down whatever you are inspired to write.

But verbalization alone, even combined with professional treatment or therapy, does not have the power to bring the depth of change and healing in our habits, relationships,

---

2   Bridget Murray, "Writing to Heal," *Monitor on Psychology* 33.6 (June 2002), 54.

and circumstances that God's Word and the sacraments do. "For the word of God is living and active, sharper than any two-edged sword, piercing to the division of soul and spirit, of joints and marrow, and discerning the thoughts and intentions of the heart" (Hebrews 4:12).

As you linger daily with the Holy Spirit over all that has surfaced in your heart and mind through his Word, verbalize what you think he is saying to you. Talk to him freely about your thoughts and feelings. Write it all down as best as you understand it and ask him to confirm or deny what you believe he is saying. Anticipate and watch to see how he answers by surveying the events of the day and week. In doing so, you imitate the Creator.

THE WORD OF GOD CREATES

When God was creating and building the physical life of the cosmos, he used his Word: "And God *said*, 'Let there be light'; and there was light" (Genesis 1:3, emphasis added). Later, as he began spiritual re-creation, he again used his Word:

> In the beginning was the Word, and the Word was with God, and the Word was God. He was in the beginning with God; all things were made through him, and without him was not anything made that was made. In him was life, and the life was the light of men. The light shines in the darkness, and the darkness has not overcome it. (John 1:1–5)

The principle is, God uses his Word to create and re-create, to construct and re-construct. In fact, the Jewish people still understand the first chapters of Genesis to be God's "housebuilding." The cosmos, Eden, the tabernacle, and later the Temple are each considered a "palace" for God. The Scriptures speak of creation in terms of the cornerstone, roof, and foundation, pillars, windows, doors, and gardens—all construction metaphors. "And God saw everything that he had made, and behold, it was very good" (Genesis 1:31). God is always creating and building; he is always speaking.

Because you are created in the image of God, you can also build and create in his image and likeness. Through LOVE the Word, through your prayer and reflection in the Scriptures, you will primarily build a spiritual edifice, or "castle," as Saint Teresa of Avila called it. We build our souls, our families, our marriages, our relationships. We co-create healing and restoration and life in our realms of influence.

All of this *must* happen from a position of prayer with God's Word if it is to bear fruit that will last. How will you know what to do or *not* do in a specific situation or relationship if you aren't listening to God and talking to him about it?

What if our verbalization with God is busy creating something else too? And what if it turns out to be a work of art?

WE CO-CREATE THROUGH THE WORD

In his letter to artists, Pope St. John Paul II encouraged our efforts to give birth to what God communicates to us in prayer:

> None can sense more deeply than you artists, ingenious creators of beauty that you are, something of the pathos with which God at the dawn of creation looked upon the work of his hands. ... Captivated by the hidden power of

sounds and words, colours and shapes, you have admired
the work of your inspiration, sensing in it some echo of
the mystery of creation with which God, the sole creator
of all things, has wished in some way to associate you.

... Every genuine inspiration, however, contains some
tremor of that "breath" with which the Creator Spirit
suffused the work of creation from the very beginning.
Overseeing the mysterious laws governing the universe,
the divine breath of the Creator Spirit reaches out to
human genius and stirs its creative power. He touches it
with a kind of inner illumination which brings together
the sense of the good and the beautiful, and he awakens
energies of mind and heart which enable it to conceive
an idea and give it form in a work of art.[3]

If this is true in a secular sense, how much more so in the
fruit of my prayer?

Like Mary who gave birth to the eternal Word, in my
own verbalization I am meant to co-create and incarnate
something. What will it be?

THE CREATIVE POWER OF VERBALIZATION

Once we have listened to the Word in the daily readings of the
Mass, the psalms of the Liturgy of the Hours, or the mysteries
of the Rosary and have observed how God is speaking through
our daily circumstances and issues, we are inspired to act,
question, thank, or rail. For Isaiah such inspiration was
a "burning coal" in the mouth (Isaiah 6:6-7); Jeremiah
called it "a fire" in the mouth (Jeremiah 5:14). All of it is
prayer with the Word. In David's and Mary's examples, their
verbalization was a co-creation with God for our benefit:
their verbalization remains in Scripture to edify, instruct,

---

[3]   John Paul II, *Letter to Artists* (April 4, 1999), nn. 1, 15, vatican.va/.

equip, and mature us (see 2 Timothy 3:16-17). Madeleine L'Engle, in her *Reflections on Faith and Art*, observed and noted the mystery of co-creating with God: "When the words mean even more than the writer knew they meant, then the writer has been listening."[4]

Verbalizing our prayers in writing is mostly a comprehensive spiritual, emotional, and mental "deposit" through which we process events and circumstances with God. It may lead to serious formal writing and it may not. The writing may turn out to be more than what we thought it meant at the time and it may not. Many times in my own prayers I wrote things that were not particularly inspirational at the time but later turned out to be prophetic or spiritually insightful in ways I know had little to do with me at all. Although such writing is not on the same level as Sacred Scripture, which is "inspired" (2 Timothy 3:16), meaning *God-breathed*, the mysterious sense of being informed by my writing never ceases to surprise me when it occurs, as I hope your writing inspires and surprises you.

The point, however, for praying like Mary with LOVE the Word is simply that we verbalize to God what we believe he is saying to us at the time, asking him to grant us the petitions he has inspired us to ask.

But what if we are more visually than verbally oriented? Can we communicate with God through visual art, too?

Recently I led a weekend retreat at which a very beautiful, very young woman sat cross-legged in the front row.[5] While

---

4 Madeline L'Engle, *Walking on Water: Reflections on Faith and Art* (Wheaton, IL: Harold Shaw, 1980), 22.

5 Georgia Morff, whose weblog, "The Esther Effect," is available on YouTube, at youtube.com/.

others verbalized by taking notes, I saw that she seemed to be merely "scribbling" through my entire first talk. I thought she was doodling, or taking notes, but when my talk was over, she showed me this drawing in her notebook.

She said the rainbow-colored balloons are my promises from God (the fruit of my prayer) filled with the helium of the Holy Spirit. As I receive and obey them, I offer them to others, and they lift and refresh (watermelon) all who hear me (Pac-Man ghosts at the bottom). I was floored. I was touched. I was baffled. I was uplifted. I was encouraged. What a gift![6]

---

6   Find more on how to visualize with LOVE the Word at biblestudyevangelista.com.

Like David's psalms, like Mary's Magnificat, like Georgia Morff's precious drawing, the world needs what you co-create with God in prayer with his Word. Verbal or visual, private or publicly shared, what God gives you in his Word must be expressed back to him. It must be born, and borne, so it can return to him: "So shall my Word be that goes forth from my mouth; it shall not return to me empty, but it shall accomplish that which I intend, and prosper in the thing for which I sent it" (Isaiah 55:11).

The *V–verbalize* step in LOVE the Word helps you pray back to God what you believe he has said to you in his Word. When journaled, these prayers will give you a tracking device that makes his voice and message clear over longer periods of time, especially when he doesn't seem to speak directly to you every single day.

You do not need to be a poet or artist to communicate with the Holy Spirit through verbalization *or* visualization. However you speak to him, he will transform negative perceptions and images and assist you in negotiating difficult relationships and circumstances. Next, we *entrust*.

LET'S REVIEW

Let's review how to verbalize like Mary.

- *The Lord confirms his Word* to Mary through her relationship with Elizabeth and the pregnancies they both experience.

- *Mary verbalizes through a song of praise and thanksgiving,* modeled on her knowledge of the Hebrew (Old Testament) Scriptures.

- *Mary's song is called the Magnificat,* meaning *magnify* in Latin.

- As David's "prayer journal" is preserved for us in the book of Psalms, *Mary's Magnificat is preserved for us in the Gospel of Luke and the liturgical prayer* of the Church.

- *As Scripture, these songs of praise teach us how to pray.*

INVITATION

One of the most difficult challenges in attempting to pray like Mary is wondering if what we're hearing is really God's voice. Elijah also had a discernment crisis, and it's one we can all learn from. Let us pray.

GOD PROMPT
Practice LOVE the Word®

L–Listen

"And there he came to a cave, and lodged there; and behold, the word of the LORD came to him, and he said to him, 'What are you doing here, Elijah?' He said, 'I have been very jealous for the LORD, the God of hosts; for the sons of Israel have forsaken your covenant, thrown down your altars, and slain your prophets with the sword; and I, even I only, am left; and they seek my life to take it away.' And he said, 'Go forth, and stand upon the mount before the LORD.' And behold, the LORD passed by, and a great and strong wind tore the mountains, and broke in pieces the rocks before the LORD, but the LORD was not in the wind; and after the wind an earthquake, but the LORD was not in the earthquake; and after the earthquake there a fire, but the LORD was not in the fire; and after the fire a still small voice. And when Elijah heard it, he wrapped his face in his mantle and went out and stood at the entrance of the cave. And behold, there came a voice to him, and said, 'What are you doing here, Elijah?'" (1 Kings 19:9-13)

O–Observe

F | Franciscan

Take a walk outdoors and see if you can hear the Lord in the wind.

I | Ignatian

Using all your senses, imagine yourself in this scene as the Lord passes by. Hear him ask you, "What are you doing here, [your name]?"

A | Augustinian

What do you think it means for you, personally, that the Lord is not "in" the wind, earthquake, or fire, but he *is* in the still small voice?

T | Thomistic

Elijah was God's prophet, so he delivered God's word to the people. Do you find anything noteworthy about how Elijah heard God himself? What, if anything, does that mean for you?

V–Verbalize

Remembering that he loves you and that you are in his presence, talk to God about the particulars of your *O–Observe* step. You may want to write your reflections in your journal.

E–Entrust

May it be done to me according to your Word.

Chapter Five

Step 4: E-Entrust

Beyond words or images is an inner silence that draws me into the great, dark rest that is God. This great consciousness shines secretly from the deepest recesses of my soul and is the source of my being.

Once your spirit has risen above the typical, mundane awareness to *listen*, *observe*, and *verbalize*, you enter the silence within and connect to the Person beyond the heavens who "knows" and guides as the Source and end of all being. Learning to pray like Mary using LOVE the Word® fosters an understanding of the world based on God's goodness. You will be able to discern patterns and unity where confusion and chaos reigned. You will find yourself cradled in a Love so powerful that you are able to risk everything to obey it. You will feel the breath of eternity on your cheek; your fear and self-concern will gradually abate and finally be swallowed up in the deeper reality that our Christian mystics point out: "All shall be well, and all shall be well, and all manner of things shall be well."[1] You will see yourself, every circumstance, and every relationship and encounter as part of something bigger, something that really *matters*. You will have left the matrix, the illusion, for the Reality.

---

[1] Julian of Norwich, *Revelation of Love* (New York, NY: Bantam Doubleday Dell, 1996), 55.

Eternity is not enough to plumb such depth.

Our doctors of prayer tell us the final, unitive stage of prayer is reaching this harmony; they say it is the prelude to heaven. This sense of profound peace is called the peace that passes all understanding in the Scriptures (see Philippians 4:7), and it can occur every day when we pray like Mary. Entering this harmony of rest, touching this deep silence, is your last step in LOVE the Word, and it is how you *entrust*.

The Trappist monk Thomas Merton spoke of a point at the center of our being that is

> untouched by sin and illusion, a point of pure truth, a point or spark which belongs entirely to God, which is never at our disposal, from which God disposes of our lives, which is inaccessible to the fantasies of our own mind or the brutalities of our own will. This little point of nothingness and of *absolute poverty* is the pure glory of God written in us, as our poverty, as our indigence, as our son-ship. It is like a pure diamond blazing with the invisible light of heaven. It is in everybody, and if we could see it, we would see these billions of points of light coming together in the face and blaze of a sun that would make all the darkness and cruelty of life vanish completely.[2]

As human beings, of course, we are not God, nor do we become divine. But as we move toward the quiet center where complete entrustment like Mary's occurs, the soul is drawn closer and closer to God. As the *Catechism* states, "Those in whom the Spirit dwells are divinized," one with him by communication and participation (see CCC 1988). According to the saints, experiencing God is not earned or even guaranteed, but is offered on his terms and by

---

[2]   Thomas Merton, *Conjectures of a Guilty Bystander* (Trappist, KY: Abbey of Gethsemani, 1965), 155–156.

his invitation, through our complete detachment, heroic charity, and a regular offering of ourselves to him in the silence of our hearts. We can practice drawing near to the mystery every day during the *E–entrust* step of LOVE the Word. God is where the soul rests. To entrust is to search out and connect to the silence that is the source of your being at your innermost soul, beyond all words and images.

The ability to entrust is what helps you see *inside* your neighbor and helps you give birth to renewal and restoration in the world, the way Mary did. You begin to understand the bigger picture: your life is not about you—it is about those you encounter today. You see yourself in your neighbor and give yourself to her and for her in whatever way the Holy Spirit within you calls you today through his Word. Like Jesus, you are broken and spilled out for your neighbor in ways that do not diminish but nourish and fill you.

WHAT IS FAITH?

But how is this practical? What does it really mean to entrust? What is faith?

How do we trust God in and for what he has given us in prayer through his Word?

As you listen to the Word—at Mass, in Bible study, on *The Bible Study Evangelista*, or while praying the Rosary or the Liturgy of the Hours, however you receive the Word of God on a daily basis and maybe in more concentrated ways on a weekly basis (as in a community study)—you want to be sure that once you have heard it, you can interpret it properly by observing your circumstances and your daily events and relationships. You want to pray it back to God as best you can, the best you know how, and the best you understand it. And then you have to entrust the consequences and everything that concerns you back to him.

The most perfect example of entrustment I know is Mary. Although I initially knew little about her, as I came into full communion with the Church I clutched her hand the whole way, identifying completely with another woman who heard a Word from God and obeyed it with a complete self-donation prior to her husband's knowledge or approval, and who entrusted the consequences of her obedience to God.

ENTRUST EVERYTHING TO GOD

As I mentioned earlier, when God speaks *to* us, he is speaking *about* us. But sometimes the Word we receive involves our relationship with someone else, as Mary's involved Joseph.

As I became convinced of the truth of Catholicism and the need to enter full communion with the Church, I assumed that my earlier call to ministry and all my promises from God would necessarily be canceled; I knew my husband would be so stunned and hurt I was likely to end up divorced. All of that was true, but God required me to lay those worries and consequences on the altar and entrust them to him.

Maybe the Word you receive is not so extreme. Maybe, rather, once you have been through the self-knowledge process with God and removed the log from your own eye (and only then), the speck in your brother's eye waves at you. Most of the time in a case like this, the Lord wants you to leave the speck with God to resolve. Usually God shows us such a speck so we can avoid the sin ourselves and pray for our brother: "If any one sees his brother committing what is not a deadly sin, he will ask, and God will give him life for those whose sin is not deadly" (1 John 5:16). This is a promise: if you see a brother or sister or neighbor sinning, then you should pray for them, because God will give them life for that prayer. Some commentators believe that John is specifically talking about mortal sin (sin unto death, sin not unto death). But sometimes you see, out of common sense, a path that a person should take or avoid, maybe one of your children or grandchildren or a friend. But God does not necessarily want you to point it out; he wants you to pray about it and leave it to him. If or when he needs you to act, he will let you know.

FAITH IS NOT MERE BELIEF

To entrust what we have seen and heard in the Scriptures back to God is faith. If God has told us to do something or stop doing something, we do it or stop it. If he has not, we do his will, whatever that is. Faith, then, as Mary illustrates it for us in the Annunciation, is active. It is not mere belief in God or in a set of teachings, or the deposit of faith of the Church. Mere belief is not faith, according to the Bible, for "even the demons believe—and shudder" (James 2:19). Demons know the truth without loving what they know through obedience.

Perhaps it is best to examine what it means to *entrust* through what theologians call a "negative approach," in which we attempt to understand what a thing *is* by looking at what it is *not*. Like white paint chips set side by side, compromised whites become more obvious beside a stark lack of color.

Entrusting *equals* faith. So what is faith?

FAITH IS NOT THE ABSENCE OF LOGIC OR REASON

Hebrews 11:1 gives us the clearest description of faith in the Scriptures: "Faith is the assurance of things hoped for, the conviction of things not seen" *Assurance* means proof or conviction: faith eventually proves that what was unseen was real all along. *Conviction* means reality or essence: faith treats what is intangible, what is hoped for, such as salvation, as confidently as what is already tangible reality. Faith provides substance in our minds to what we hope for and anticipate and makes it present to us before it comes to pass, and it does this in a way that has us obeying and following before we see the fulfillment.

But to *entrust*—that is, to have a living, active faith—does not involve suspension of logic or reason. When God reveals something, and we believe it upon the divine and infallible authority of the revealer, we have a greater certainty of it than any demonstration can afford us. For "God is not man, that he should lie" (Numbers 23:19). Instead, faith lays hold of what the senses and reason are unable to grasp.

In his doctoral thesis, *Faith According to St. John of the Cross*, Pope St. John Paul II points out that the proper function of faith is as a means of union with God. Faith is necessary, he says, because "the intellect naturally seeks the essence of things."[3] But the essence of God is pure spirit. His essence is spirit. There is nothing to see or hear or sense of him at all unless he makes himself felt or seen or heard. Human beings receive information through the senses.

---

3   Karol Wojtyla (later John Paul II), *Faith According to St. John of the Cross*, trans. Jordan Aumann (Eugene, OR: Wipf & Stock, 1981), 82.

Since God is pure spirit, and therefore beyond sense, he must be received and "reached" through faith. The intellect searches for the essence of God Who is Spirit, but it "terminates in darkness"[4] because Spirit is intangible: faith is the only way to "lay hold of" God. Because logic and reason are the product of the brain's interpretation of sensory information, logic and reason cannot be the sole arbiter of faith.

However, logic and reason remain important. So God reveals himself, his purposes, and his ways to us through his Word. He gives us tangible external proofs, "motives of credibility" (CCC 156) according to reason, that inform our faith, so that faith becomes "man's response to God, who reveals himself and gives himself to man" (CCC 26). As faith seeks understanding, it leads to greater knowledge of God. Greater knowledge calls for deeper faith. So faith and reason work together as we *entrust:*

> By *faith*, man completely submits his intellect and his will to God. With his whole being man gives his assent to God the revealer. Sacred Scripture calls this human response to God, the author of revelation, "the obedience of faith." To obey (from the Latin *ob-audire*, to "hear or listen to") in faith is to submit freely to the word that has been heard, because its truth is guaranteed by God, who is Truth itself. (CCC 143–144, original emphasis)

Our Lady most perfectly embodies the obedience of faith. By faith Mary welcomed the promise of the Word of God brought by the angel Gabriel at the Annunciation, believing that "with God nothing will be impossible" and giving her assent: "Behold, I am the handmaid of the Lord; let it be [done] to me according to your Word" (Luke 1:37–38).

---

4   Ibid.

Elizabeth celebrated with Mary as she greeted her: "Blessed is she who believed that there would be a fulfilment of what was spoken to her from the Lord" (Luke 1:45). For her faith, the whole world in all generations since has called Mary blessed.

Throughout her life and until her last ordeal when her son died on the Cross, Mary never ceased to believe in the fulfillment of God's Word, for which the Church venerates in her as the purest realization of faith (CCC 148–149).

Mary's faith was not in the logic of God's Word to her through the angel, since a virgin birth was illogical and still is, according to the science we have currently at our disposal. Mary also teaches me that to entrust does not mean putting faith in my faith. Faith is not doctrine. Mary's faith was not in the mere practices of Judaism— the frequency or fervency of her prayers; her love for, discipline in, or faithfulness to Israel's practices; or the potency of her belief. Mary's faith was in God's Word, to which she entrusted herself completely.

FAITH IS NOT PUTTING FAITH IN OUR FAITH

Years before I entered the Catholic Church, I taught a tightly knit adult Sunday School class in my denominational church. An older couple in our class discovered they were pregnant late in life, and we all anticipated their baby's arrival with thrilled excitement. Two days after his birth, it became clear the baby boy was dying. Huddled in anxious knots, our entire church took turns sitting and crying with the parents while praying and fasting for three days, but their baby died. Their agony and confusion were devastating to all of us.

Several months later, we welcomed a new family to our church, and the adults began attending my Sunday School class. Clearly, they had come from a "prosperity gospel" background, which proposes that sickness and poverty are curses of sin, while health and wealth are God's reward for faith.

One Sunday when the baby's beloved parents were not in class, I led a prayer for them and scheduled meals and visits to help support them in their continued grief. During the discussion, "prosperity gospel" gentleman commented that the baby died because of his parents' lack of faith. The rest of us became so angry it was necessary to ask him to leave.

Common sense tells us it cannot be true that we only have to have enough faith to get what we want. In every town and government in the world, it is plain that poverty does not mean people are evil or are being punished by God, just as riches and power do not equal faith in God. Having "enough" faith is not the same as truly entrusting ourselves to God.

Sometimes we think we only have to have enough faith, and God will do a specific good thing for us, but this is ultimately an attempt to manipulate God. Mary did not attempt to manipulate God; she entrusted. She did not put conditions on the Word she heard: "Let it be [done] to me according to your Word" (Luke 1:38). Mary left circumstances open ended: "Do whatever he tells you" (John 2:5).

To entrust, then, is not a matter of having faith in faith, in its correctness or measure. Trust is not a matter of having enough belief in what you want to happen so that God will do what you want. Faith must be grounded in God's goodness, no matter what happens.

If you are in a tragic place, if you are suffering deeply, be comforted in knowing you are not suffering because you have too little faith; suffering is a result of the Fall. Accepting that God's ways are not necessarily our ways, even in little things, is a process. We do not usually arrive at such an understanding and acceptance the minute or even the year that tragedy strikes. Grief is a long process. We work out our salvation in fear and trembling (see Philippians 2:12). We struggle toward working out what happens after God says no.

To entrust does not mean "having enough faith." Jesus said, "If you have faith as a grain of mustard seed … you will say to this mountain, 'Move from here to there,' and it will move" (Matthew 17:20), but the Church Fathers say he was not quantifying our faith so that we would get a mountain of what we want. Rather, he was saying that the power of true entrustment is such that mountains will move: mountains of barrenness, grief, challenge, problems, tragedy. We cannot make God do what we want. Instead, we allow God to be God.

FAITH IS NOT TRUSTING IN WHAT WE WANT

Have you ever found yourself trusting God to do some "spiritual" thing you are convinced he needs to do? What comes to mind is a particular friendship I have with a long-term atheist. Her mother went to church regularly and spoke often of her personal faith in God, but she died in a tragic car accident when my friend was in high school. My friend was devastated and swore off faith and God from that point on. She once told me that for her to have faith in God she would have to experience a miracle.

Certainly, although she would be offended, I continue to pray for her life-changing, soul-saving miracle every day at 3:00 PM. Surely it is God's will that she come to know him personally for herself and be healed of her loss. But year after year, my friend is colder and colder toward things of faith, and toward me personally as a person of faith. Of course a miraculous conversion would be a powerful witness of God's love and a testimony to his tireless pursuit of her and each one of us. I would be thrilled to see it occur. Maybe it will.

There are many things we would love to happen simply because they seem to be in God's best interest, but just because something would be "great for God" or for another person does not mean it will happen. Therefore, we should not entrust ourselves to that desire, however holy and meritorious it is.

Nor should we entrust ourselves to what we desire in a particular circumstance. I recall watching an intervention on television in which alcohol and drug issues, pornography, and materialistic extravagances existed in a family that didn't attend church. The woman's faith resided in her husband's ability to provide lavishly for her, which he did by selling drugs. When the marriage fell apart and her teenagers rebelled, she was devastated to the point of nervous breakdown. Her faith was in her husband's intention and ability to provide a life that looked successful and happy, whether they were actually successful and happy or not. When the extent of his cheating became known and she realized her life had been built on sand, she fell into a total alcoholic tailspin. The entire extended family's fervent prayer was for her to go to and succeed at rehab, but it was many, many years later before she did, and it was largely unsuccessful.

Maybe you know someone in a similar situation and you're praying that they will have a conversion experience and begin going to church so that things can improve. We pray this way because we know God "desires all men to be saved and to come to the knowledge of the truth" (1 Timothy 2:4).

But we cannot put conditions on what *should* happen when we are entrusting a prayer, relationship, or situation to God. Although we may know that faith is an expression of utmost confidence in God, we may mistakenly impose our own ideas of the best outcome rather than truly entrust the situation to him. Such an error can happen even when we have heard a specific word from him in the Scriptures regarding a situation, because we have no idea of the methods or people he might work through. Rather than assume or cajole, Mary teaches us to ponder and wait.

We must not entrust ourselves to what we think God should do rather than to God himself. We must not put faith in our faith: "I have faith, I go to church, so God should, or is going to, do this for me." We must not entrust ourselves to a particular outcome. We should hope for but never invest faith in what we *want* to happen, or count on what we think *should* happen. Every person has free will to choose. Mary did not have a faith that said that God had to act in a particular way. She said, "Do whatever he tells you" (John 2:5).

Faith is not trusting in what we want to happen. Entrusting is having faith in him, and that is all.

FAITH IS NOT MY ABILITY TO KNOW GOD'S WILL

To entrust is not to have faith in our ability to read God's will or know what his will is.

When I first began practicing LOVE the Word, my husband and I were looking for permanent living arrangements. We considered buying and building a home. In my morning prayer time I read Matthew 21:1: "And when they drew near to Jerusalem and came to Bethphage, to the Mount of Olives, then Jesus sent two disciples." One town away from us was a town called Bethpage! We looked at houses, but nothing in the area met our needs, so we searched for houses in the paper, and instead of a house, we found an upcoming land auction in Bethpage. Because of the Scripture reading, I was convinced we were supposed to buy that land and build there, so when we did not win a bid, I was embarrassed and confused by how wrong I had been. I learned I should not trust my emotions or first inclinations, and instead should look for confirmation and patterns when reading and discerning God's voice.

Oddly enough, later we did move to Bethpage. But even when we are convinced God has said something to us through LOVE the Word, we cannot put our faith in even that. I think of the prophets throughout the Bible who heard from God and preached on his behalf, but their prophecies always came true much differently than expected and always over a longer period of time than it seemed at first. I believe God does this on purpose, because as soon as we get a Word from him, we begin trying to own it, planning how to make it happen, often forgetting that the initiative and the plan are God's prerogative.

Throughout the Scriptures, when his people received a Word from him, he immediately removed all their supports; "it" does not happen for a long time, and certainly not in predictable ways. God does not want our faith to be in the thing or the circumstance or the person. He wants our faith to be in him alone. He will remove every impediment to pure faith, the faith that is truly in him and him alone, because pure faith is built on a relationship with him. God values your relationship with him far more than anything you want from him.

When painful or difficult things happen, even devastating things, we determine to be strong and have faith. For many people, "having faith" means being positive. And positivity is certainly better than negativity. But in my experience God lets me go as far as I can possibly go with positivity, and then he shows me beyond any shadow of a doubt that there is no hope without him. He exercises my faith muscle to *increase* my faith, to make new things possible. He does this because he loves us. He is not punishing.

When we do break (for me, that means I lose it and lash out), we should not be discouraged or punish ourselves, because the entire experience is a pop quiz. We are learning.

God gives us opportunities to practice what we hear from him about our relationships, habits, and circumstances. Through pop quizzes, which are unique to each of us and our lives and needs, he purifies incomplete and imperfect faith, so we can see for ourselves what we are and how imperfectly we love.

Mary's faith was not in her ability to be strong or stoic in difficult circumstances. She entrusted herself to whatever

God allowed, and to his goodness in and through her circumstances. Her faith was in God's will, not her ability to predict his will, because God is unpredictable, as the prophet Daniel and his friends also experienced.

Daniel and his friends Shadrach, Meshach, and Abednego were thrown into the lions' den because they would not worship Nebuchadnezzar's idol. Daniel stood firm:

> If it be so, our God whom we serve is able to deliver us from the burning fiery furnace; and he will deliver us out of your hand, O king. But if not, be it known to you, O king, that we will not serve your gods or worship the golden image which you have set up. (Daniel 3:17-18)

Daniel and his friends, and every martyr of faith after them, show us that faith is not trusting in our ability to know God's will. Whether he saves us immediately or not, here or in heaven, they say, we still will never worship your idol. Amen.

The enemy attempts to divert our faith. He wants us to have faith in our faith. He wants us to have faith in a particular outcome. He wants us to have faith in how long we can have faith. He wants us to have faith in our ability to know what God's will is. But God wants our faith in him, because he is the only One who will last. Whether it happens the way we want it or not, we will serve God.

FAITH IS NOT A FEELING

True faith, then, is an act of will. Most of us allow emotion to drive the train of our spiritual lives when the engine of faith resides in the will. I like to say faith is the engine, emotion is the caboose.

Intuition and emotion certainly have a legitimate role. But as we practice praying like Mary, I reiterate what the Church's doctors and theologians have taught for millennia: there's nothing to see, hear, sense, or feel of God at all unless he somehow takes a form. God is pure, uncreated Spirit. Invisible, except in Christ. If we "feel" him at all, it is because he makes himself felt. Our emotions, then, are insufficient and unreliable guides in determining God's movement and voice. We listen, observe, and verbalize; we watch to see how he works so we can join him there; and then we entrust every consequence and outcome to him.

Negative emotions are often from the enemy, as we see in Hebrews 3 and 4, where fear is equated with unbelief. But according to the doctors of prayer, soaring excitement or feelings of closeness can be temptations presented by the enemy as well—temptations to pride and presumption through wonderful experiences. Emotion must always be measured by God's Word, read with the mind of the Church. We trust what *he* says, and we trust in his love for us.

Whether God does what I want or not, I will serve him. Whether I get what I determine I need in a particular situation, or someone else gets what I determine they need, I do not entrust myself to that discernment or logic. My faith is in the goodness of God.

That is what Daniel teaches us.

That is what Mary teaches us.

Christians are not more holy because they believe certain events will take place or because they have identified (or think they have) what God wants them to do. The account of

Daniel and his friends shows us that believers are not more "faithful" when they think they know what God will do next.

Sometimes Christians try to prove their faith to themselves or others by predicting God's actions. One example is end-of-the-world predictions. Another is the election of a new pope. People sometimes lose their faith entirely because they think God or the Church or the pope should do this or that, and when what they want or think should happen does not, they walk away. Others link their faith to reading circumstances through the filter of providential insight or private revelations; some trust in Catholic personalities. Still others believe that speaking in tongues or offering prophecies or some other outward sign is proof of strong faith. But God does not usually guide us through the immediate gratification of emotional, exterior displays. Instead, the Bible teaches that God takes the long view in stretching, deepening, and growing our faith.

ENTRUSTING MEANS LONG TERM

Sometimes God cannot tell us everything there is to say about a circumstance in one day, especially if we are only spending five minutes reading the Gospel. We must take the long view with him. Many of our circumstances drag on for months or even years. Guiding us through them is not something he can do in one sitting or even one week. Additionally, it is important to keep verbalizing back to God what you think he is saying over time, because you may get mixed signals.

When you get what seem like contradictory messages, it becomes important that you have also kept track of all you have heard on a daily basis, so that you are not confused.

Is he saying this or that? I have learned that sometimes it is actually both. In some of my own circumstances, I came to realize in the back-and-forth confusion over weeks that it was not one thing or the other; it was both things.

We often have difficulty holding two seemingly contradictory things in our hearts and minds at once, but God loves paradoxes and works through them: faith *and* reason, Scripture *and* Tradition, free will *and* election, faith *and* works—not one or the other but *both*. If I am not paying attention to and observing my circumstances closely, I may not catch that God is working in a paradox, in which two opposite things are happening at once that make one unified thing!

Conflicting messages are a normal part of discernment and entrustment. Maybe you have been longing for a family member to come home to the Church, and you receive such a promise from him in his Word. What if it has not yet happened, although you have been waiting? Perhaps over a long period of time God renews the promise, and yet there is no evidence, or maybe there is even evidence to the contrary?

Probably you are being encouraged to wait and persevere, as all the heroes of faith were, through the contradictions of faith (see Hebrews 11). In these cases, writing down your *V—verbalize* step is important for long-term tracking of what you hear.

The test of whether or not something is really a word from God is whether or not it comes true. And even when a word to you from God *does* come true, whether through the Scriptures or another person, chances are it will not be at the time or in the way you first imagined it would come to pass, if the examples of God's heroes of faith are any measure (see Hebrews 11). We can be confident and hopeful, but never presumptuous. The Bible warns against putting our faith in wealth, in strength, or in anything whatsoever but him.

HOW TO ENTRUST

Knowing some of the "names" God's people gave him in the Bible is important, because they give us confidence to call on him when we need him. The third commandment, "You shall not take the name of the Lord God in vain," is most often applied to cursing or similar abuse of God's holy name. Blasphemy and taking a false oath in his name, as in perjury, are also meant (CCC 2142–2155).

In the Scriptures, "vanity" is consistently used to illustrate worthlessness, emptiness, or futility (see Ecclesiastes). Most of us would not think of using God's holy name as a curse word, but we do often render it empty in our own lives by neglecting to turn to him and trust him for help. Therefore, taking the Lord's name in vain can also be a sin of omission, something we do *not* do when we should.

When we need his help (salvation) but neglect to call on the name of the Lord, his name lies empty for us. We do not know it or experience it, and so we render it fruitless for ourselves.

To "trust in the name of the Lord," to entrust through LOVE the Word, is not mere belief. We do not suspend reason or logic or trust merely in dogma and doctrine. To entrust is not to put faith in what we want to happen. Nor is it to trust in our ability to read God's will.

Faith, quite simply, is trust in God alone, in his name, in *who he is.* It has been said that we must "let God be God." Biblical faith lets God be God. The LORD, the I AM, does not depend on our effort or our view of what he should or should not do. We must trust in the name of the LORD, entrust ourselves to the truth that God *is* God and he is trustworthy, no matter what.

The most difficult, purest tests of faith are those times when God's answer is no. When the one we love dies. When there is no miracle. When a relationship gets worse rather than better. When we are oppressed and persecuted. When tragedy strikes. When the fallen-away Catholic or the wayward child does not come home. And all the while you have done your part, going to church, praying, receiving the sacraments, living a godly life. Everyone, at some point in his or her life, becomes disillusioned in the faith because of another Christian or a scandalizing circumstance, even while praying with all fervency toward a silent heaven. Is your faith still in God when the answer is *no?*

I pray your answer is just the mustard seed of a *yes.*

When we use the LOVE the Word method, we practice *entrusting* all listening and observing and verbalizing back to God. Mary teaches us to entrust ourselves to the Word in this way. "Let it be [done] to me according to your Word" (Luke 1:38), no strings attached. Blessed be the Lord, who only does wondrous things (see Psalm 72:18). God is good, all the time. Amen.

LET'S REVIEW

Let's review what it means to entrust the way Mary practices it.

- *When I hear a Word from God, I entrust* the consequences and all that concerns me back to God.
- *To entrust means to put my faith in God* himself.
- *Faith is not mere belief*, for even the demons believe and tremble.
- *Faith works with logic and reason to increase my knowledge and experience of God.*
- *Faith trusts that God is who he says he is*, and is not a matter of quantity or measure.
- *Faith is not trusting in my faith, in what I want to happen, or in my ability to predict God's will.*
- *Faith is a matter of will*, not of positive feelings or positive thoughts.
- *"Every one who calls upon the name of the Lord will be saved"* (Romans 10:13, emphasis added).
- *Faith is choosing to trust* God's timing, God's provision, and God's rest in every circumstance.

INVITATION

In our careening culture of economic stress, widespread depression and anxiety, high pressure, and chronic busyness, we consider rest to be a luxury. The Bible teaches, however, that rest is a spiritual discipline that requires us to entrust all that concerns us and all consequences to God's love. Our Doctor of Prayer, St. John of the Cross, encourages persistence: "Seek in reading and you will find in meditation; knock in prayer and it will be opened to you in contemplation."[5] Let us pray.

GOD PROMPT
Practice LOVE the Word®

L–Listen

> "Therefore I was provoked with that generation, and said, 'They
> always go astray in their hearts; they have not known my ways.'
> As I swore in my wrath, 'They shall never enter my rest.' Take care,
> brethren, lest there be in any of you an evil, unbelieving heart."
> (Hebrews 3:10-12)

---

[5]   John of the Cross, saying 158, in Kavanaugh and Rodriguez, *Collected Works,* 97.

After reading the Scripture passage, choose one of the following approaches:

O–Observe

F | Franciscan

Choose one thing you can do this week to make your Sunday more restful. Put a plan in place to practice this for the coming weekend. Consider making it a permanent practice.

I | Ignatian

Part of entering the promised land of rest is leaving behind what is lost, what is already behind and gone, things we continue trying to find and carry with us. Who or what are you willing to let go of and give back to God?

Imagine you are walking through a lovely meadow of flowers, with birds, sun, and breeze all around. As you walk, you sense a presence beside you that is warm, safe, welcoming, wise, and loving. … It is Jesus who walks with you. As you walk, you see a figure, someone or something, becoming visible in the distance. As you and Jesus draw closer, you see it is someone or something you have lost. Who or what is it?

Now, with Jesus by your side, you may say everything in your heart. You may express everything you were not able to before or after the person or thing was gone.

When you have said it all, visualize yourself and Jesus continuing on the path, leaving this person or thing behind. You take a few steps and turn to bless him, her, or it. What do you say?

A | Augustinian

What circumstance in your life has God pointed out through this passage? Where are you distrusting his timing, his provision, or his rest?

T | Thomistic

Spend some time identifying the who, what, where, when, why, and how of the Scripture passage. Then find the same elements as they relate to your own life. Who is God speaking to you about? What is the circumstance? What have you done or not done? Where do you go next? When should that happen? Why does he ask this of you? How will you carry out his wishes?

V–Verbalize

Remembering that he loves you and that you are in his presence, talk to God about the particulars of your *O–observe* step. You may want to write your reflections in your journal.

E–Entrust (*May it be done to me according to your Word!*)

Perhaps you'd like to take a few minutes to simply wonder in the extraordinary promise of God's salvation and provision, and entrust yourself to him anew.

Chapter Six

Love Gives Birth to the Word in the World

As Mary entrusts her heart to God in love, he entrusts his Word to her, and she gives birth to that Word in the world, entrusting him to me and you.

What, then, is praying like Mary through LOVE the Word® meant to produce? As Catholics we have a unique appreciation for Mary's prayers, and we naturally desire to imitate them, if not for their intimacy with Christ, then surely for their efficacy and longevity. In following LOVE the Word, we imitate how our Blessed Mother prayed. In fact, perhaps *How to Pray Like Mary* is her invitation to a new intimacy with her in union with the Holy Spirit, and a new power in prayer.

As Catholics, we listen to the Word with the mind and heart of the whole, ancient Church, beginning with the first Christian. As Pope Emeritus Benedict XVI stated, "Mary shows us the right way to come to the Lord. She teaches us to approach him in truth and simplicity. Thanks to her, we discover that the Christian faith is not a burden: it is like a wing which enables us to fly higher."[1] Mary's

---

[1] Benedict XVI, Angelus, September 14, 2008.

Annunciation teaches us "the right way to come to the Lord," the ultimate model of prayer with the Scriptures.

THE JOYFUL MYSTERIES

When we pray the Rosary, we enter Mary's prayer through the Annunciation, when Mary hears the word of God through the angel. In the second mystery, the Visitation, she ponders it as she travels, observing the circumstances and people involved. Then she prays it back to God in the presence of Elizabeth, who confirms the Word for her, and Mary's Magnificat remains, two millennia later, the prophetic song of Evening Prayer for the whole Church.

The third mystery, the Nativity, finds Mary giving birth to Jesus, the Word she received from the angel. She cradles the Word, now incarnate, in her arms, and prepares to offer him to the whole world. Later, at the Presentation (the fourth mystery), she submits and offers her Word back to God in the Temple, where he confirms it and elaborates on what to expect through the prophets Simeon and Anna, who rejoice in God's faithfulness to his people. In the fifth mystery, the old law is fulfilled with the arrival of Christ, the final Word of God, who is found in the Temple when he takes his place in his Father's house as the true and final temple.

Following Mary through the LOVE the Word method is so much easier than through *lectio divina*. When most people first attempt *lectio* they cannot remember the Latin or the steps, so they get frustrated and give up. Travesty! Latin is a silly thing to get hung up on. So we follow Mary's love for the Word using a method that grew out of my meditation on the observations of Pope Emeritus Benedict and Pope Francis, that Mary is the "model for prayer" and the "mother of listening." The LOVE the Word method is fruit from Church history's prayer with the Annunciation and the other Joyful Mysteries of the Rosary. In hearing and accepting Mary's personal invitation to enter into and understand the way she prays, I can offer my own little word to the world. And so will you.

FEASTING FROM THE ONE TABLE

The "one table of the Lord," the *Catechism* tells us, is both the Eucharist *and* the Scriptures. This is why Jesus offers himself to us in the Mass in two parts, the Liturgy of the Word and the Liturgy of the Eucharist. If we are only feasting from one half of the table, we are missing a great deal of the nourishment he intends for us:

> The Church has always venerated the Scriptures as she venerates the Lord's Body. She never ceases to present to the faithful the bread of life, taken from the *one table* of God's Word and Christ's Body. In Sacred Scripture, the Church constantly finds her nourishment and her strength, for she welcomes it not as a human word, "but as what it really is, the word of God." "In the sacred books, the Father who is in heaven comes lovingly to meet his children, and talks with them." (CCC 103–104, emphasis added)

This quote from the *Catechism* is a convenient synopsis for what the Church teaches about the Scriptures, but one of the things that is strongly emphasized in Church teaching is that the Word of God comes to full life within the liturgy of the Church—specifically, the Mass. The Mass readings are very important for learning to love the

Word and hear from God in the Scriptures on a daily basis. As mentioned earlier, the lectionary is the set of readings for each Mass of the year. Free and inexpensive resources for the lectionary abound.[2]

I read morning prayers, Mass, and evening prayers plus a meditation in Magnificat magazine every day. If you are unable to pray the longer prayers of the Liturgy of the Hours, the daily fixed-hour prayers that our holy orders and religious pray, just try the lectionary. Remember that God speaks to us every day through his Word in the Mass readings, spoken to the entire Church throughout the world. So join the chorus and make an effort to at least read the Gospel (which only takes five minutes) every day for forty days.

I recently returned from a book tour in Poland, where all of my books have been published in Polish, a very difficult language to learn. Using the Order of Mass and daily readings in my Magnificat magazine, I was able to follow along with all of the readings and prayers, even recognizing names and other Words in the readings, despite knowing only a handful of Polish words. What a thrill to be connected to every Catholic in the world through the Word of God every day! When I came into full communion with the Church and first realized God was speaking directly and specifically to me, individually, through the same readings he was speaking to the whole Church at the same time, I was absolutely floored all over again.

---

[2]   You can find the daily Mass readings in print in Magnificat magazine (us.magnificat.net), Give Us This Day (giveusthisday.org), The Word among Us (wau.org), and Living Faith (livingfaith.com). They are offered online by the United States Conference of Catholic Bishops (usccb.org), EWTN (ewtn.com), Universalis (universalis.com), and Blessed Is She (blessedisshe.net), and are available on the Laudate app for your phone or tablet.

CONCLUSION

To love the Word like Mary, to listen well, to allow the Word its wild reign in us, and to offer the fruit of our listening to those who are still struggling to hear require a fullness of grace. Like our "mother of listening," God is always calling us in his Word to do what in the world's eyes is impossible. Instead of saying "I can't," we can simply reply with her wisdom: "Be it done to me according to your word." Just like Mary, we approach the Word every day, and ask the Holy Spirit to speak: *Come, Holy Spirit.*

"Today, if you hear his voice ... " Today, still, every day, I LOVE: *Listen*, *Observe*, *Verbalize*, and *Entrust*. As I go to the LORD in the Scriptures on a daily basis, I can use this helpful acronym to discern his activity and will and *listen*, there, to his voice. I *observe* my relationships and circumstances for pop quizzes and patterns and notice how they confirm and connect to the word I receive. I *verbalize* back to God my thoughts and fears and feelings about all of it, what response I think he desires from me, what I believe he wants me to do. And I fully *entrust* all that concerns me to him for the long term, no matter how long it may take.

"The word of God is living and powerful ... " (Hebrews 4:12). As I love the Word the way Mary, "mother of listening," teaches me to, Scripture comes alive in my reality. I bring the power of God's Word to bear on my relationships and circumstances, and as the Word begins to take root and thrive in me, I experience God in prayer in ways that make me a giver of Christ to the world with Mary. With her, I become a long-term disciple of Jesus, who changes the world, and not simply a haphazard pray-er or church-goer: "If you continue in my word, you are truly my disciples" (John 8:31).

AS YOU GO FORWARD

It thrills me more than you can ever imagine to know that some of you will begin in the Scriptures for the first time with LOVE the Word because of this book. If you have difficulty establishing a practice, please do not give up. Stay with it, and it will become a necessary habit that will change your life forever.

If you started once and were not able to continue, please start again. I beg you. I know that God will speak to you. The Bible is full of the promises and assurances. He will heal you and lead you if you continue with him.

I hear God speak through LOVE the Word. I began in my twenties and continue today. It's not some quaint little ditty for me. I use it. I live by it. I would be crazy without it. In listening, observing, verbalizing, and entrusting the events of my life, I am able to see that God has been leading me through a long process.

I am not special. He will do the same thing for you.

LET'S REVIEW

Here's how to pray like Mary with LOVE the Word.

- *Mary teaches me how to pray,* as the mother who taught the Incarnate Word, our "model for prayer" and "mother of listening."

- *Mary knew Scripture, and her daily prayer was shaped by it.*

- *The Bible is half of the "one table" of the Lord* (CCC 103).

- *"All Scripture is inspired by God and useful for teaching, for reproof, for correction, and for training in righteousness"* (2 Timothy 3:16).

- *"Ignorance of the Scriptures is ignorance of Christ"* (St. Jerome).[3]

- *As the "model for prayer," Mary teaches me how to pray* with the Scriptures.

- *Mary guides me as I learn to pray with LOVE the Word.*

- *The LOVE the Word method means* listening, observing, verbalizing, *and* entrusting.

---

3   Thomas P. Scheck, ed. and trans., *St. Jerome: Commentary on Isaiah* (New York: Newman Press, 2015), 1.1.

INVITATION

For the rest of your life, you are invited to a daily encounter with Jesus, Word of God made flesh, as an event of grace that runs through the reading and the hearing of the Sacred Scriptures. As the Church reminds us, "each person needs to hear like Mary and with Mary, the Mother and Teacher of the Word of God."[4]

Praying like Mary with the LOVE the Word method is not meant to confine you to a rule. Rather, it is a guide to an encounter with lifelong freedom in the Scriptures. Mary always leads us to encounter her Son, and she models this freedom for us in approaching him as the Word.

In the following passage from John on the wedding in Cana, notice that Mary demonstrates the LOVE the Word steps but in a different order. First, she *observes* a need. Then she *listens* for what the Holy Spirit wants her to do about it. She goes to the servants to prepare them to receive the answer, then she *verbalizes* and *entrusts* the need to Jesus.

Even now, Mary continues to love the Word in any order necessary to bring us to him. Let us pray.

---

[4]   Synod of Bishops, *Instrumentum Laboris*, The Word of God in the Life and Mission of the Church (May 11, 2008), 26.d, vatican.va/.

GOD PROMPT
Practice LOVE the Word®

L–Listen

"On the third day there was a marriage at Cana in Galilee, and the
mother of Jesus was there; Jesus also was invited to the marriage,
with his disciples. When the wine failed, the mother of Jesus said to
him, 'They have no wine.' And Jesus said to her, 'O woman, what
have you to do with me? My hour has not yet come.' His mother
said to the servants, 'Do whatever he tells you.'" (John 2:1-5)

O–Observe

F | Franciscan

Throw a LOVE the Word party in which you eat and drink with
merriment, and practice LOVE the Word together using the
passage above. Encourage those invited to bring a journal, either
a notebook from home or perhaps specifically a *LOVE the Word
with Mary* journal. Remember to read the passage aloud, observe
individually and silently in the group, verbalize by writing down
thoughts and feelings that arise and (for those who want to) by
sharing with one another, and pray the prayer of entrustment
(below) together.

I | Ignatian

Mary smiles when the bride and groom look shyly at each other
while reclining with their families and friends around the feast, all
villagers for whom the wedding is a welcome celebration. The fig
on Mary's tongue dissolves in a final burst of earthy sweetness, as

cheerful as the laughter, good wishes, conversation, and prayers swirling about the festive tent.

Sheltered within exquisite fabrics, the celebrants are all sparkling with wine and mirth, enjoying their reprieve from laboring in pastures and groves and vineyards. The sumptuous fruit of their labor spills off platters onto the brightly woven rugs, in piles of olives and grapes, pomegranates and figs, lamb and fish. Even Jesus' face, still a little gaunt and shadowy around the eyes from his recent forty days in the desert, is rosy with celebratory wine. Mary pats his rough carpenter's hand, happy to be with him as he enjoys the camaraderie of his disciples and friends, and her stomach growls when she inhales the spicy scent of roasting meat.

Twirling the fringe on her cushion, she reaches down to plump the wool for a better position. Mary remembers the tenderness of her own promises to Joseph and the sweetness of their time together. She sighs with a prayer of gratitude for the beautiful gift of marriage: *What a glorious image of your love for us*, she prays with double meaning, glancing again at Jesus.

Distracted from the party by her reverie, Mary sees the subtle flash of concern when the steward leans in a little too closely to serve a loaf to the groom's father and whispers delicately in his ear. An embarrassed glance out the back of the tent, and Mary knows. She pauses.

And now she feels the first twinge of Simeon's prophetic sword, for if she implores Jesus' help, she knows his life will never be the same. From this day forward, for better or worse, in sickness and in health, till body and soul are parted by death, his mother knows he will never refuse when asked to provide, or heal, or teach, or save, or suffer, or give. He will always say yes, because he is the yes of the Father.

Yet if he meets this need for wine supernaturally, the quiet seclusion of his life will be over, and the new wine of a New Covenant will begin its spill from the earthen pitcher of this Galilean Jew, her beloved son. Looking poignantly at the host and then at Jesus, she weighs this last moment, the moment when the pendulum of their time together will have swung to its furthest arc, and Mary knows there will be no turning back.

But it is for him to decide.

Her role is simply to bring him the need. Resisting any obvious display of affection, she leans over to place the gentlest whisper in his divine ear, and rises with only the slightest tremor to prepare the servants to receive their savior: "Do whatever he tells you."

A | Augustinian

What is the wine you need? Who is depending on you for wine? Is the laughter beginning to wane? Have you hoped the wine you had could be stretched by watering it down or only filling the chalice half full? Are you down to dregs at the bottom of the wine vats? What has Jesus said to you about who satisfies this need?

T | Thomistic

Spend some time thinking about the cause and effect in this passage. What do you think the cause and effect of LOVE the Word could be in your life? Spend some time with the Holy Spirit formulating a goal in this regard.

V–Verbalize

Ask Jesus, *What if I need a miracle, Lord?* How does he respond? You may want to write your reflections in your journal.

E–Entrust *(May it be done to me according to your Word!)*

Come, Holy Spirit, fill the hearts of your faithful.

Enkindle in them the fire of your love.

Send forth your Spirit and there shall be a new creation.

And you will renew the face of the earth.

O God, who by the light of the Holy Spirit did instruct the hearts of the faithful, grant that by the same Holy Spirit we may be truly wise and ever enjoy his consolations, through Christ our Lord, Amen. +

Dear Reader,

Mary is inviting you right now to consider your life through the lens of the Annunciation, to hear the Word of God speak to you through his incarnate Word in ways that make you a bearer of him into the world.

Mary has been showing us how to love the Word since before Jesus was born.

With Pope Francis, I pray that you accept her invitation and welcome God's Word into your heart every day for the rest of your life. "May Our Lady teach us to welcome the Word of God fully ... in our whole life."[1]

Sonja

---

[1] Francis, Address to the Italian Biblical Association (September 12, 2014), vatican.va/.

Appendix

Additional Ways to Connect with LOVE the Word®

LOVE the Word is a simple method of prayer, simple enough for you to practice every day, simple enough to share with and teach your children, your grandchildren, your neighbor, and your RCIA and other religious education classes.

You can practice LOVE the Word with a group, as the Franciscan part of God Prompt in chapter 6 illustrates, perhaps in a weekly meeting at your home or your parish or as a prelude to a study or meeting. Read a passage aloud for the group, possibly the Gospel reading for the coming Sunday. Allow everyone time to observe silently. Share aloud with one another to verbalize. Pray a prayer of entrustment.

As mentioned in chapter 6, there are innumerable resources in the Church today for finding the readings—websites, phone apps, magazines, and podcasts—so there is no excuse for not praying like Mary every day. Consider also listening to the Word of God more intensely through my weekly radio series, *The Bible Study Evangelista Show,* "Bible study spinach that tastes like cake." This continuous Bible study series on the Word of God is available also as podcasts on my website, on the Laudate app, in iTunes, and everywhere podcasts are found. You can do your daily readings and then also get a big dose for an hour once a week at your convenience.

You can also join the thousands who redeem their Mondays with LOVE the Word meditations each week. Your LOVE the Word devotion arrives via email every Monday morning with an audio teaching of the current series from *The Bible Study Evangelista Show*. The email also includes a written LOVE the Word exercise according to each of the FIAT prayer temperaments we discussed in chapter 3; a free, printable LOVE the Word journal page and guide; a semi-weekly teaching video; and all the relevant references, notes, and resources. Sign up for free on my Bible Study Evangelista website, biblestudyevangelista.com, or on the profile picture of my Facebook page, Sonja Corbitt.

Because we should all be in the Scriptures on a daily basis, my whole ministry is dedicated to making it as easy as possible. So I created an annually themed *LOVE the Word with Mary* journal that comes out every January.

You might consider taking your LOVE the Word or other journal to Mass. Prepare for Mass with this thought in mind: "Holy Spirit, what do you want to say to me?" This preparation is so important that I include it in the instruction guide in the *LOVE the Word with Mary* journal. The Holy Spirit is always speaking. What that short prayer really does is make us attentive to his voice. Prepare for Mass with that short prayer, then *listen* for God's voice in the prayers, music, readings, and homily. Something will catch your attention. Note it quickly in your journal and then later, after Mass, use it to practice the other steps of LOVE the Word: *Observe* your life and relationships for ways to put his Word into practice. *Verbalize* by writing your impressions in your journal. *Entrust* your day or week to the Lord.

Share the LOVE with me on Instagram and Facebook under Sonja Corbitt or Bible Study Evangelista, where we all use #LOVEtheWord and #LOVEtheWordtakeaway to share the LOVE with one another and the community as we mine the treasures God offers us every day in the Scriptures.

Our LOVE the Word practice is a private expression of love for and trust in God, as well as a public expression of a historical faith. In order to pray like Mary, to love the Word as she does, we immerse ourselves in Scripture on a daily basis, and we pray with it using LOVE the Word for at least a few minutes every day. I pray that you will experiment with your schedule, establish the habit, and stick to it.

As Mother of God and Mother of the Church, Mary prays in and with the Church at every decisive moment of salvation history. Let us entrust to her every moment of our own lives, and let her teach us the need for such prayer, so that in loving union with her Son we may implore him for the outpouring of the Holy Spirit and the spread of the Gospel to all the ends of the earth.